Writing with Kindergarteners

Lessons from the Emerging Learner

Kim Dumaine-Banuelos

Book Two: Kindergarten

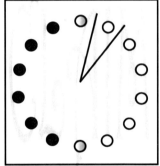

Curriculum for Literacy and Implementation Modules

Writing with Kindergarteners

Lessons from the Emerging Learner

Kim Dumaine-Banuelos

foreword by
Glenda L. Bissex

Spring, TX ♦ New York

Copyright © 2012 Kim Dumaine-Banuelos

All rights reserved. No part of this publication may be reproduced, transmitted, or stored in an information retrieval system in any form or by any means, graphic, electronic, or mechanical, including photocopying, taping, and recording without prior written permission from the publisher.

ISBN 978-1-888842-39-5

Printed in the United States of America

Requests for permission to make copies
of any part of the work should be mailed to:

Permissions
Absey & Co. Inc.
23011 Northcrest
Spring, Texas 77389

Visit us at www.Absey.biz

To Janet Emig

Table of Contents

Foreword—viii
Preface—x
Introduction—1
Chapter One—Four Day Drafting Cycle—5
Chapter Two—Get Those Babies Started—11
Chapter Three—Prewriting
Chapter Four—Family Writing—30
Chapter Five—Responding to Literature—38
Chapter Six—Response to an Author—46
Chapter Seven—How-To Writing—51
Chapter Eight—Descriptive Writing—57
Chapter Nine—Writing Narrative Birthday Stories—61
Chapter Ten—Writing Narratives—68
Chapter Eleven—Writing Letters—74
Chapter Twelve—Writing in Subject Areas—81
Chapter Thirteen—Publishing and Celebrating—109
Chapter Fourteen—Assessment—113
References—117

Foreword

When my son was in kindergarten, there was no writing curriculum—although he wrote plenty at home. I'm delighted to be invited into Kim Bañuelos's kindergarten room where writing is so encouraged. The roots of this encouragement matter, for they are not ambition to push children "ahead," but her own love of writing and her well-founded belief in children's capabilities. A highly conscious teacher, she always shares the reasoning behind her pedagogical decisions. While this book reads like a rich resource guide of writing activities for young children, Kim's spirit is a more essential model than any particular activity.

In her classroom, writing is not a separate subject to be learned but a skill integral to all subjects—literature, math, social studies, science. Talk about writing across the curriculum! Talk about an integrated day! Such practices are just natural parts of Kim's writing teaching. Of course the children write about all sorts of things—writing is part of their lives. And all of that writing is reading material for the writers themselves and for their classmates. What a reading program! (In addition to the many trade books that feed into the children's writing.) Kim's writing lessons teach social as well as academic skills—listening to one another carefully, responding thoughtfully, working together in small and large groups, gradually assuming independence in their work.

Kim doesn't label herself a teacher-researcher, but clearly she is. In concluding this book, she writes: "The experience of documenting a portion of this last year's writing lessons has truly been a joy for me. I have sincerely been able to view the growth of my students from an enlightened point of view. I loved watching my students grow, learning from my mistakes, gaining ideas and insights from my students, and learning side by side with my Kindergarteners."

We get to watch Kim as she reflects on and revises her teaching, When her students' writing begins to sound formulaic, for example, she analyzes and experiments with her assignments. When her new approach still doesn't lead to individual enough voices, she does what the best teachers and teacher-researchers do--she consults the kids. Together they solve the problem. "I know that I can always go to my kids to straighten me out." That takes trust and courage.

Kim values the children's individual voices just as she values her own voice and creativity as a teacher. When faced with mandates, she finds ways of fulfilling them that do not compromise her teaching or her students' enjoyment of learning. She works with teachers, staff and administrators beyond her classroom to help celebrate student writing.

So even if writing isn't your thing, and even if you don't teach young children, you still have much to learn from Kim Bañuelos's Kindergarten.

—Glenda L. Bissex

# Preface

CLAIM: Curricular Literacy and Implementation Modules

In March of 2004, following the NJWPT (now Abydos Learning International) Teachers' and Trainers' Annual Conference, where influential Board of Directors of Abydos Site Directors continued to point out the one gap in the project was implementation, we began work to establish a CO-MISSION of trainers who would represent grades Pre-K through 12. We declared it a "CO" mission, not a "Commission" because we wanted to emphasize its work as one with an equality of purpose.

Invitational letters were sent to fourteen handpicked NJWPT/Abydos Trainers for this important goal. All accepted. With us as directors, we referred to this group as CO-MISSION SIXTEEN. Sixteen of us made it our mission to help young, in-coming, inexperienced teachers and those who loved the institute but who were in a quandary about exactly how to implement it, work it into their stated curricula, or integrate the project's principles, strategies, and philosophy into their day-to-day classroom agenda.

Our initial meeting, held September 4, 2004 at the Hotel Sofitel in Houston, boasted a core group of enthusiastic trainers representing thirteen disparate districts across the state. Since we all agreed our purpose centered on the importance of implementation, we tackled how to research, design, and launch this mission. We asked ourselves: What common sources could we all read? What would be the best way to share our collective expertise? How best could we share our methods of implementation? What title might we use for our work?

After grappling with a host of acronyms ranging from CLIMB: A Curriculum for Literacy Implementation and Model Building to ACCLAIM: A Content Curriculum for Literacy and Implementation Model to our favorite CLIP: A Curriculum Implementation Plan, we dismissed some for negative connotations, others were "taken," still others we felt were not quite on target with our mission, and a few were too cumbersome or wordy. This terrific group of CO-MISSION members finally unanimously chose CLAIM: Curricular Literacy and Implementation Modules.

We liked that the word *claim* suggested ownership, something we wanted each teacher to experience, grab on to, and hold. We liked the specificity of the words *literacy* and *implementation*. We really liked the word *modules*, suggesting standards, dimensionality, the sense of interchangeability, as well as units of instruction.

We brainstormed, researched and finalized the following sources for all of us to read:

Caine, Renate Nummela and Geoffrey Caine. *Education on the Edge of Possibility.* Alexandria, VA: ASCD, 1997.

Glickman, Carl. "Pretending Not to Know What We Know." *Educational Leadership,* 48 (8) 4-10, 1991.

Hall, Gene E. and Shirley M. Hord. *Implementing Change.* Boston: MA: Allyn & Bacon, 2005.

Jersild, Arthur T. *When Teachers Face Themselves.* NY: Teachers College Press, 1995.

Joyce, B. and Showers, B. "Improving Inservice Training: the Message of Research." *Educational Leadership,* 37 (5), 379-385, 1980.

So we had self-imposed homework to do.

We envisioned a series with a book for each level written by teachers who teach and implement NJWPT/Abydos on that level. We decided to engage colleagues to share in this process through input, feedback, and support. We also wanted to produce videos (still a possibility) so teachers could see implementation in action. To that end, and perhaps ambitiously, we invited a tech expert to our next meeting.

Between 2004 and the first phase of publishing, we met at least once in the summer, several times at the NJWPT/Abydos retreat, and always at the conference. In between these times, cadres met. For example, the Pre-K through first grade met, or the third, fourth, and fifth grades met.

Then we hit our first snag.

The trainer committed to write the twelve grade book moved—not just districts but out of state. We had to find another trainer. Then it happened again. This time the trainer committed to the ninth grade book entered law school. We had to find another trainer. A third trainer became a principal, and although she maintained her commitment, her new position impinged upon her time. A fourth took a position in another district as a curriculum coordinator, but she had worked ahead of time and actually was the first trainer to complete her book.

We were flexible. Deadlines came and went—and we realized our desire to have thirteen books published in one year, thirteen books to be launched at a single conference was not to be. So we regrouped and decided to introduce the books in phases. Phase One, then, would come out in 2008 with subsequent phases in subsequent years.

Throughout the process, we all grew. We listed possible items for the modules—twenty-two to be exact—we discussed the vocabulary of concept, strategy, activity, tactic, and we reviewed levels of lessons. We contacted parents and students for permissions, took pictures, made videos. We studied and contacted authors for Forewords, each of us sharing in the joy when one us received a letter from our "author" agreeing to write a colleague's Foreword. Some even entertained the idea of an Afterword. Most of all we remained cohesive and energized.

So after four years of study, hard work, camaraderie, and lots of writing, we offer you this book of phase two in the series CLAIM: Curricular Literacy and Implementation Modules. We hope you learn from, through, and because of it. We hope this book and this series helps you make NJWPT/Abydos come as alive in your classroom as it does in ours. We have gained so much professionally and believe we are doubly validated because our work will grow exponentially through you and your students. Know that all lives you touch directly or indirectly will be enhanced because of this undertaking.

May the process be with you……

Joyce Armstrong Carroll, Ed. D., H.L.D. Co-director, NJWPT/Abydos Learning

Series Authors:

Jimmie O'Quinn, Pre-K, Spring Branch ISD
Kim Dumaine, Kindergarten, Richardson ISD
Valerie Sosa, First, Pflugerville ISD
Natalie Hoskins, Second, Friendswood ISD
Robin Johnson, Third, Lovejoy ISD
Bobby Purcell, Fourth, Amarillo ISD
Jodi Hughes, Fifth, Austin ISD
Suzy Lockamy, Sixth, Northside ISD
Michelle Jackson, Seventh, Granbury ISD
Steve Kelly, Eighth, Edinburg ISD
Mona Robinson, Tenth, Pasadena ISD
Dottie Hall, Eleventh, Northside ISD

Introduction

I was blessed early. During student teaching, I worked under Jana Hoffpaiur, a gifted Abydos/NJWPT trained kindergarten teacher. I remember speaking to her on the phone about a week before my assignment began. Mrs. Hoffpaiur said to me, "All teachers have a particular thing that is important to them. Mine is writing……..well, you'll see." And I did see. I saw that Writer's Workshop was the meat of her day. Her thematic units revolved around getting kids to write. She protected her kids' writing time no matter the assembly, the fire drill, or administrator coming in for in visit. She taught me loyalty to the children. She showed me that every student could write, and more – that every student wanted to write. Jana let me watch and conference with children in kindergarten who could write independently for thirty minutes and still want more time. Jana fed the beliefs that were already inside of me. She knew my soul, although she may have never known that she did. Jana believed in kids. And she believed in me. She gave me a cliff to jump off, and believed that I could fly. My hope is that she is now able to see that I followed her flight plan.

In turn, I believe in young children. I believe they can be smart, hard working, and dedicated to a craft. I believe – I know – that even five year olds, can be inspired. Kindergarten children are smart, confident and capable writers. Not only do they write for fun, they write to share what they learn, to send a message, to give instruction, or to record information. I also know that kindergartners love writing, and even become addicted to writing as adults do – especially when my five-year-olds ask if they can bring their journals outside to write during recess!

As is the case with most teachers, I taught several years before I came to those revelations. (I had been teaching in a private school for years before I returned to college to receive my Early Childhood Specialization, during which blessed time I met Jana Hoffpauir.) I regret the years that I taught before I became 'turned on' to the abilities of children. But I know those years had a purpose for me, as I often run into teachers, parents, and administrators, who do not yet know and understand the capabilities of young children. I can relate to how they think and feel, since I used to think and feel the same way. Hopefully now, I can shine a spotlight on these capable young children, and the wonderful gifts they have to offer.

In fact, I did not make writing a priority in my Kindergarten classroom until 1999. That was the year a whole new world opened up to me. Because of writing, I grew to know my kindergarten students on a much more intimate level. This caused me to care for more students more deeply. Because of the writing process, we morphed from a classroom of kindergarteners plus one teacher, into a community of learners that worked together and truly cared for one another. Most teachers who have taken part in the Three-Week Writing Institute offered by Abydos Learning International and have implemented its philosophies and strategies have experienced this phenomenon. When we conference together, we share a part of our souls. When we respond to one another's writing, we form a deep appreciation for one another. A bond grows. We want to hear the growth of each other's pieces. We become concerned about one another's stories. We care about the progress of our friends' pieces, and we want to listen and discuss each new revision.

The same thing happens in the kindergarten classroom. Kindergartners meet with friends to discuss stories. They talk even as they are writing. They help each other "say the sounds" when a friend is stuck on a word. Children tell each other ahead of time how their stories are going to "end up." I conference with them, and they conference with me. And we bond. Through writing, we become a second family. We learn what is important to each other. In turn, this causes the children to want to write even more and even better! 'I know that my audience wants to hear my writing, and this makes my writing even more valuable!' they seem to say through their enthusiasm.

In her book, **GNYS at WRK,** Glenda Bissex shares that her own son, Paul, "became a fluent writer (using his own spelling system) before he became a fluent reader" (viii). I believe this to be true of many young children, as it has typically occurred in my own kindergarten classrooms. I believe this occurs because children have greater control when they are themselves the author, saying the sounds that they hear in each word, and recording them on paper as they say them. This may appear to take place in a limited way to the adult eye. The young writer may not include every single letter that we expect to see in a word, but the child is writing. Even the child who writes with controlled scribbles, or uses random strings of letters or even uses picture to write, is writing.

In this early stage of school life, it is extremely important that writing be given the same time and concern as all of the other subjects. I recently had a representative from a scripted reading program say to me, "Children can not write until they can read." This broke my heart and made me sad for the children that are now being 'taught' with this program. Writing helps to grow readers. When young children write, they are, in fact, teaching themselves to read better. They are slowly breaking down the words as they write so that they learn the sounds well enough to put them into text. They are working at a higher level — applying their knowledge! Writing is best taught side by side with reading. The two are intertwined intimately. What wise teacher has not introduced a writing concept with a read aloud? Good teachers know that writing is married to reading. Children know it in their bones. How many times have we all seen young children take a well-loved story and craft their own versions, perhaps naming "me," as the new main character?

As a teacher of young children, I encourage my students to write for themselves, and for the purpose of using writing as an instrument in learning. I am careful not to stifle their desire to write with my own need to control errors in their writing. Richard Gentry says it best. "Very young children should be encouraged to invent their own spellings as a way of testing and modifying hypotheses about spelling. This is the way children learn"(9). I need to allow my children that freedom.

Doing so not only creates better writers, but better (and more confident) readers as well. About her son, Bissex wrote, "Paul described what he was doing as "writing" rather than "spelling" (35). She later shares, "He cared about what he writes, not just how he wrote it" (35). This is the way that I want my students to write. Beginning writers always start out with a purpose. They have a message, and I do not want to change that mindset in my young writers. I want my students to want to write, as Paul did. Like Paul, I want each student to write, "because what he was writing had meaning to him as an individual and as a cultural being. We humans are meaning-making creatures, and language – spoken and written – is an important means for making and sharing meanings"(107). Paul was indeed a blessed child to have a mother as wise as Glenda Bissex. I want to give my own students the same independence, freedom, and confidence that Paul received.

To do all of this, I must offer myself as a facilitator, or a guide to my students as they write. I must be a hands-on teacher with my young writers. I must do more showing and less telling. I must model, model, model, and then model some more. As Judith Newman says in *The Craft of Children's Writing*, "Children don't need to be told how to write; they need to be shown…By providing demonstrations of writing in action, by being partners in the creative process, we do more to help children figure out how to be writers themselves than all of our correcting their 'mistakes' can ever hope to accomplish" (106). This is my goal as a teacher of young writers. I must constantly remember that the experimenting that my children do with their writing will lead to future risk-taking. I want them to be risk-takers. I want them to love Writer's Workshop each day. I want my students to write because they want to write, because they love to write, and because of all that writing has to offer them. I want them to write to increase their learning, to become more confident, and to gain self worth. After all, writing has done all of these things for me. I do not wish to keep this gift all to myself —it deserves to be passed along.

Not only do I want to instill a love for writing into my students, but I also want to challenge them. This means that I must know each child well. This requires an investment of my time and energy. This is an investment of self. Each child in my class is developing at a different level from the next. I must keep up with their milestones and with their accomplishments, as well as with their needs. And I must be willing to aid and direct each child as the need rises. In *Children's Minds*, Margaret Donaldson advises, "Thus a very important part of the job of a teacher (or of a parent while in the teaching role) is to guide the child towards tasks where he will be able objectively to do well, but not too easily, not without putting forth some effort, not without difficulties to be mastered, errors to be overcome, creative solutions to be found" (120). To achieve this goal I need to know which of my students is in need of a little nudge, and exactly when that nudge is required. This is not easy, but as Carroll and Wilson state in the Fall 2005/Winter 2006 ***Reflexive and Extensive Journal***, "Writing is hard work. Teaching writing is harder work" (6). True. And it is work born out of love. Love for the students. Passion for a craft. And faith that the hard work has its rewards.

My hope is that, through the work of my students, I can share the times when a student needed a little nudge. I can also share lessons that have worked and ideas that got children excited about writing. The lessons included in this book are simply examples extracted from a year in my kindergarten classroom. They are by no means comprehensive. More so, they are simply a sampling of lessons that may have inspired my kindergarten students to become happy writers. Every lesson may not work for every teacher or even every child. Even in my own classroom, every child did not always choose to write using the lesson that I modeled. Often times, I model some strategy or skill, only to have a handful of my kids say, "I really just want to write in my journal today," or, "I'm still working in my draft book right now." And that is just fine with me. Self-motivated writing is the richest writing. Most of all, my hope is to share that young kids are bright, capable, gifted writers.

I am happy and proud to be a teacher of young writers. The rewards come daily through my students. And I am happy and grateful to be a NJWPT trainer. The knowledge that I have received from. Carroll and Wilson has forever changed my belief system about children and my belief system about myself as a teacher. "NJWPT holds firmly that writing and reading are processes that must be nurtured, taught with joy, verve, and knowledge, processes that need time and consistency" (Carroll and Wilson 6). This is my guiding principle as I teach writing to my five-year olds. I will never reach perfection as a teacher. But the joy I witness at my students' triumphs gives me reason to unlock that classroom door each morning, knowing it will be a good day.

Four-Day Drafting Cycle: Why Writer's Workshop?

I have heard teachers question

why kids need to experience Writer's Workshop at such a young age. This is understandable, since many schools, including my own, do not have a Pre-Kindergarten program, and thus, most of our Kindergarten students come into Kindergarten with no writing skills at all. Most of the students enter without the letter/sounds relationships mastered, and they do not know how to form letters. I once had a first grade teacher ask me, "Where is all this Creative Writing coming from? Shouldn't we be teaching the kids penmanship and formation of the letters?"

My personal belief is that we can teach formation of the letters, and letter/sound relationship as a part of Writer's Workshop. I use my Writer's Workshop time to reinforce those exact skills, even though I may have also taught them during a different time of the day, such as during Word Work (which may include phonics, making words, and similar activities). So actually, my students are receiving a double dose of the skills I want them to master. And Writer's Workshop gives the student greater control of their own learning. When a child says a word slowly to listen for the sounds, that child becomes his or her own teacher of both writing and reading. Children put more effort into working when they have greater control and are able to make choices in their writing. Rather than just having children copy a word or copy a sentence, as many scripted literacy programs would have them do, Writer's Workshop allows the CHILD to choose the sentence they want to write, based on their own life experiences. This gives value and ownership to the student, which inspires confidence and desire to write more.

My hope is that the following examples of children's writings (Figs. 1.1-1.4) will serve as a BEFORE and AFTER snapshot. I hope that these examples will help answer the question, "Why Writer's Workshop?"

In these examples, I asked the students to write about their friends without giving them any introduction to the process of continuing to work on the same story over several days' time. You see that the date was December 1st. The writing was good, but short, sweet, and to the point.

Fig. 1.1

Fig. 1.2

Fig. 1.3

Fig. 1.4

Two weeks later I modeled a four – day writing cycle, as seen on the video. Part of the story was written by me and part was written by the students. Each day, we take turns in writing the story. One day I add a sentence, the next day the students add a sentence through Interactive Writing. Both drafting and editing are intermingled together to show that either one may occur at any time. The examples of drafting and editing are kept extremely simple for the sake of the video. (Some times when I model a draft, it ends up looking like a complete mess with lines drawn through sentences and all the carrots showing.) The students help to make decisions about my piece each day. I involve the kids in this process to ensure they fully understand they have the ability to make decisions about a piece of writing, which includes making additions, drafting, and editing all on the same piece of writing.

My purpose was to display the difference in the children's writing that occurs after the four-day process was modeled for them. The stories now (after modeling the four day cycle) read as follows:

Cale's piece Fig. 1.5-1.7):

How me and Pierce Met
We met at Pre School. I was 5. Now I am 6. So is he. We are in Kindergarten. We are working right now.

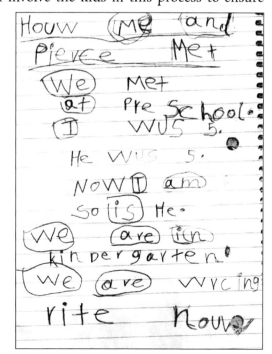

Fig. 1.5

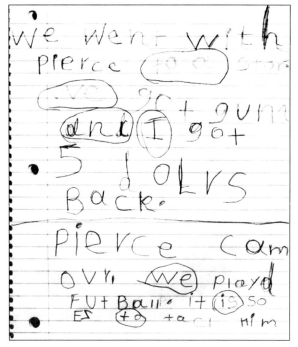

We went with Pierce to a store. We got gum and I got 5 Dollars back. Pierce came over. We played football. It is so easy to tackle him.

Fig. 1.6

We got in a big fight. Pierce hit me. I kicked him.

Fig. 1.7

Pierce's piece (Figs. 1.8 & 1.9):

I like Cale. <u>How we Met</u> I started talking to you. Then we played together. We had fun. Then we came inside. We had a drink. Then my mom picked us up. His mom was half – way down the road. His mom said he could stay. We played with my blocks. Then we ate. It was a fun day. The next day we did the same thing. That day was fun also. Cale is my best friend.

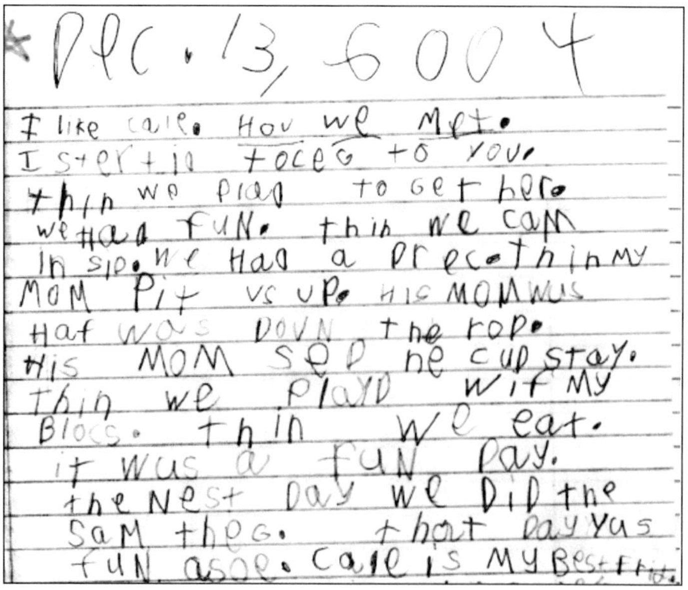

Fig. 1.8

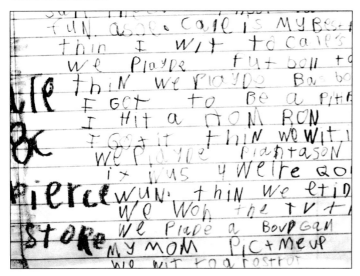

Then I went to Cale's house. We played football tackle. Then we played Baseball. I got to be a pitcher. I hit a home run. I got it. Then we went inside. We played Playstation. It was 4 Wire. Quinn won. Then we eated. We won the TV. Then we played a board game. My mom picked me up. We went to a restaurant.

Fig. 1.9

Simon's piece (Figs. 1.10 & 1.11):

At the Zoo

Me and Mojahed went to the zoo. Mojahed's favorite animal is Brontosaurus. Mojahed is a good friend.

Fig. 1.10

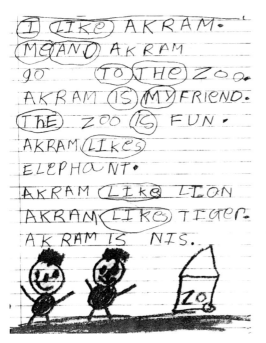

I like Akram. Me and Akram go to the zoo. Akram is my friend. The zoo is fun. Akram likes elephants. Akram likes tigers. Akram is nice.

Fig. 1.11

Katherine's piece (Fig. 1.12):

I am lucky
Rachel is my friend. Me and
Rachel sit down together at lunch.
Valerie is nice. Rachel is nice.
My friends are cool. I am lucky.
Cool! Illustrated by Katherine

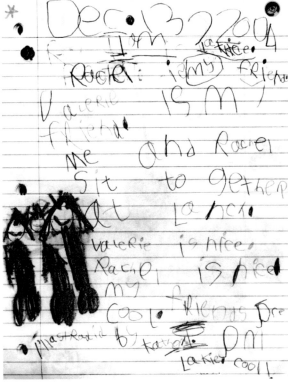

Fig. 1.12

Leighton's piece (Fig. 1.13)
:

My friend Kate
Me and Kate went to Indian princesses.
We got in my grandpa's truck. My
Friend is Valerie. She is nice. We
Play with each other hide and seek.

Fig. 1.3

These pieces have a little bit more meat than the previous set. Before modeling the four-day cycle, I saw the typical one or two sentences that were written by most of my kindergarten students. Helping the students to realize that the same story can be worked on for several days makes a big difference. Young children truly experience process writing when they return to the same piece over a series of days.

I hope that this BEFORE and AFTER snapshot of students' writing helps to show the value of Writer's Workshop in the Kindergarten classroom. In my own experience, I have found that giving kids freedom to write as they choose, combined with daily teacher modeling, produces not only better writing, but more importantly, better (and happier) writers. And as a teacher of writing, I know that I am far more interested in the WRITER. One additional benefit of Writer's Workshop is that I am able to learn far more about my students, their interests, and their personal lives by conferencing with them over their reflexive writing than I ever would by asking them to copy a sentence from a purchased literacy program.

2. Get Those Babies Started

Starting Writer's Workshop on the Very First Day of School

The first several days of Writer's Workshop will be about addressing Writer's Workshop behaviors as much as they will be about skills. These behaviors will need to be practiced over and over again until mastered. Imperative to a smooth Writer's Workshop are children who are fully aware of all expectations. (The following guidelines will simply outline my personal expectations for my own students.)

I have found the key here is to know the theory and the pedagogy, but ultimately myself well. I must decide what works well for me and my students and stick by that! It is hard work in the beginning, but the pay off is well worth it. I like to remember this motto: *More work now means less work later.* I repeat this to myself on the days that I am feeling tired. It will get better! When I am excited about writing, my students are excited about writing. Because I love writing, so do my children. I tell them that writing is my favorite time of day. I tell them that if I could not be a teacher, I would want to be an author. I tell them that I do get to be an author each day during Writer's Workshop. Letting my students experience my own joy and love for writing keeps them fired up!

You will note that I include Interactive Writing as a component in Writer's Workshop almost daily. This is a personal choice, and all teachers do not believe it to be as imperative as I do. In fact, I utilize Interactive Writing two or three times each day. Yes, it is work until I get a routine established. I just remember the motto.

Let's get started.

DAY 1:

We begin at the large group area. I assign each child his or her own personal spot. This minimizes behavior problems. The classroom should have an easel with chart paper and markers for modeling. The easel should also have a shelf with white boards for the students, dry-erase markers, and some type of erasers (I like to use tissues). I explain to the children that each day we will use markers and white boards for many things, but right now we are just going to practice passing them out. I have my children sit in rows so that I can always address the row I want to talk to by Row 1, Row 2, or Row 3. (If your room is big enough to have only two rows, or a semi circle, you may prefer such an arrangement. I think this through before the first day of school.) My intent is for the first child in each row to take a board from the top of the pile, and then pass the pile of boards to the child to the right. I explain to the children that I will pass the white boards at first. The procedure is to place the exact number of boards for each row into the lap of the first child on that row. I explain to the children, "Take the board off the top and place it on the floor in front of you. Then pass the rest of the boards to the lap beside you." Then I repeat, "Take one off the top and pass down." I ask the class to repeat, "Take the one off the top and pass down." This may seem monotonous, but overdoing the practice will only help the process. I watch as the children pass the boards, and make corrections as needed. I know the more I stay on top of things in the beginning, the easier my job will become. I remember the motto! Now it is time to pass the baskets of dry erase markers. I follow the exact same procedure as I do with the boards. Since I have three rows, I have exactly three "marker baskets." I ask the students to take a marker and pass down the basket. Then I have them repeat, "Take one and pass it down." I instruct them that if the person sitting beside them is not paying attention when the basket is passed to just place it on their lap. I ask the children to place the marker at the top of their boards until we "are ready to use it." Again, I watch closely so that I can make any corrections that may be required. The goal is that my students will quickly adapt this habit of passing every supply to the child sitting to the immediate right. I ask the very last child on each row to place the basket on the floor beside them. This will help with easy clean up later on. Last but not least, we pass the tissue boxes. Each child takes one tissue, lays it on top of the white board, and passes down the box. I repeat the "Take one and pass it down" instructions. Then I ask the child at the end of the row to place the tissue box atop the marker basket.

Now is the time to talk about attentive listening. Attentive listening teaches the students to "listen with your eyes, your ears, and your heart" (Gibbs 91). Good listeners glue their eyes to the speaker and think about what the speaker is saying. I ask the children to show me what this looks like. I realize I will have to revisit this idea many times over the first couple of weeks. I remind myself that I am doing a wonderful service for my students (and myself). I begin my first Writer's Workshop with a Reading Writing Connection. I always choose a book about self. Self is what five years olds are all about, especially on the first day of school. I like the book, *I Like ME*, by Nancy Carlson. I introduce a few of the parts of the book, such as the front cover and the title. I keep this short because this is the first day and the children are anxious. I invite predictions by asking, "Does anyone have an idea what this story may be about?" Since this is the first day of school, answers range from, "I think it's about a mouse." to "I'm hungry now." After two or three suggestions, I explain that this story is about a child who is telling us all about herself. "She is happy with herself." I read the story, stopping along the way to allow for discussion, and to check for comprehension.

After the read aloud, I announce that this book has given me an idea. I want to write about ME. I ask the children to be attentive listeners while I show them my idea. I use my own markers to draw a picture of myself. I continue to use the word ME. "If this is ME, what color should my hair be? If this is ME, what color should my dress be?" When my drawing is complete, I inform the students that I want everyone to know that this is M, and I would like to write the word ME. I invite the class to say the word ME. "Now let's say the word ME slowly so that we can listen to the sounds." We all say ME slowly. I think aloud, "I wonder what ME will start with? What letter makes the m sound?" Almost always- there is at least one child who already knows his or her letters and sounds who yells out "M!" If not, I point to the letters directly behind me (on the Word Wall) and drag my pointer along while making the m sound. Once I get to M someone figures it out. The child who calls out "M" gets to come up and write it next to my picture. Of course I act very excited about the child who is coming up. This will build the desire to participate in all of the students. I explain to the rest of the class, "You can make the M too. Use the marker in front of you to make your own M."

Occasionally I need to help the child who comes up to the chart. I hold the child's hand around the marker, and help them make the M. I do not worry about teaching proper letter formation at this time. I just let the kids know how exciting it is to be able to write the beginning sound. As a class everyone can point to their own M's and make the sound. Now I repeat the word ME. I ask, "Can anyone hear the last sound?" The child who raises his or her hand (or calls out the answer at this point) gets to come up and write the letter E next to the M. The rest of the class writes the letter E on their white boards. Next to have the students point to the word they have just written and read the word ME out loud. Finally, I ask them read the word I wrote next to my picture. I ask them to repeat the word and point to it one more time.

Excitedly I explain to the children that they will be able to write on the first page of their own "journals" today. I use spiral notebooks, but some teachers like to make books for the kids out of unlined white paper. (Use whatever you like and can store in your room.) In my classroom, each child has his or her own "journal box" which ends up housing journals, draft books, artifacts, writings-in-progress, and anything else that goes with Writer's Workshop.

"But first we need to put away our markers and boards." This time, the last child on each row is asked to pick up the marker basket, replace his/her marker, and pass the basket down for the child to his/her left on that row to do the same thing. I take up the three baskets. Then I ask the children to hold up their marker boards. After I take each child's board, that child walks his/her tissue to the trashcan and proceeds to collect his/her journals from its box. I ask all the children to turn to the first page (which I model) and "Write about yourself." Many students draw a picture of themselves on this first day of school because this is what I modeled. Quite a few students write the word ME near their pictures. Yet others will go with their heart. There is no predicting what some of the children will show me on this first page. As the students work, I walk around the room and place the date at the top of each child's page. As I do this, I can view each child's work in progress. I give the young writers twelve minutes to work. (By the second semester they can write for thirty minutes straight through.) Next I ask the kids to clean up their tables and bring their journals to the carpet. I remember that I am also teaching procedure, so I stay after those kids who loiter at the table. When all of the children are sitting on the carpet with their journals in front of them, I teach them a little cueing system that helps me. "If you would like to share today, please sit with your journal open to the page you wish to share. If you do not wish to share today, please close your journals." This allows for the shy children to pass on sharing until they are more comfortable—without calling attention to themselves.

I ask one or two children to come up to the front and share their work. I do not introduce the author's chair on the first day of school. I model asking a question about the first child's work, such as, "Who is the other person I see in your story?" Then I invite one other child to ask a question or make a comment. I repeat this process with the next child. This is a good time to explain sharing to the class. I always tell the students that everyone will not be able to share every day, but everyone will definitely get their chance to share. (Usually about four children share each day.) Then I am always certain to make good on this promise within the first week or two of school. *Acts of Teaching*, by Carroll and Wilson, offers wonderful sharing strategies. Pointing (151) invites the student listeners to point out what they liked about the author's piece. Say Back (156) teaches the students listeners to pick out ideas that they want to hear more about, which in turn, offers constructive comments for the author. Both of these sharing techniques work well in the beginning of the school year, when eliciting responses from timid kindergarteners.

The last procedure to tackle is putting away the journals. First I praise all of the young writers for their hard work, and we applaud the children who shared. Next I call the students by rows to put their journals into their journal boxes. "Row 1, put your journals away. The rest of us will watch to see if you find the correct box." I repeat with Rows 2 and 3.

Please bear in mind that you may wish to manipulate this process so that it works well for you and your students. This is by no means a prescription for a perfect Writer's Workshop. Writer's Workshop looks different in different classrooms. In fact, even my own classroom Writer's Workshop looks very different on the first day of school than it does during the last days of school. For a comprehensive view on Writer's Workshop as a whole, I suggest reading **…And with a Light Touch** by Carol Avery. She knows that there is no how-to formula for Writer's Workshop, but she is amazing at walking the reader through the process.

DAY 2:

Since I am establishing routine and procedures, I set up the second day of Writer's Workshop to look like the first. I begin with a read aloud that the kids can relate to, usually about a child going to kindergarten for the first time. Nancy Carlson has written a lovely story about this subject— **Look Out Kindergarten, Here I Come!** We stop and notice things that the main character likes to do in kindergarten. The boards, markers, and tissues are passed out exactly as they were the previous day, reestablishing the exact same expectations.

I remind the students, "Yesterday I wrote about me, and today I feel like writing about me again. The book we just read gives me an idea. I am going to write about something I like to do in kindergarten." I solicit ideas from various children, asking what they like to do in kindergarten. "I like to play outside, I like to draw," and "I like to eat lunch," are the top choices in my classroom. Choosing an idea for myself, I tell the children that I like to swing. I ask the class to say the sentence, "I like to swing" along with me. Next we clap the sentence, "I like to swing." Finally we count the words in the sentence, "I like to swing."

We are now ready to write the sentence on chart paper; the students do the same on their white boards. I ask if anyone remembers the first word. Someone raises a hand to say "I." This person comes up and writes *I* as the rest of the class does the same on their boards. I may need to help the child write the word *I* by placing my hand around theirs in order to help form *I*. Next, I ask if anyone knows the next word. The child who offers "like" may come up now. As a class we say the word "like" slowly as we listen for the beginning sound. Hopefully one or two of the students hear the beginning sound, and the child at the chart paper writes the letter *l* with or without help; I will complete the rest of the word quickly. I do not want to get too bogged down attending to the correct spelling of the word. This can lend itself to creating students who copy the teacher's writing, or students who constantly ask, "How do you spell……?" We end the sentence with the words "to" and "swing" using the same interactive writing as "I" and "like." I also draw a picture of myself on a swing.

At this point I ask the children to erase their boards because I want to talk to them about the way writing looks in kindergarten. I will tell them that all writing is good writing in kindergarten, but one person's writing may look different from another person's writing. "One person's writing may look like this." I model controlled scribbles, as described in *Acts of Teaching* by Carroll and Wilson. My example of this may include squiggly lines going across the page, or a line of circles going across a page. I will try to pull from the writing I had viewed the day before. (Fig. 2.1). "Some other people may write like this." I will show a random sampling of letters. (Fig. 2.2) "Some people may even write like this." I will rewrite the sentence "I like to swing," using only the beginning sound of each word. The writing style of every child in the class can be found somewhere in these examples. I constantly assure the students that "all of us are writers." I reassure them all of this fact as I walk

Fig. 2.1

Fig. 3.2

around the room and ask them to, "Read your writing to me." The rest of the procedures happen exactly as they happened on the first day, including cleaning up and sharing time.

DAY 3:

Like most kindergarten teachers, I do use the student's names to teach letters and sounds in my classroom. Additionally, I place the student's names throughout the classroom, including a center in which students can match photos of friends with names of friends. So on day three, I will make use of my student's names during Writer's Workshop.

As always, we begin in the large group area with a read-aloud. I begin with a story of a child making friends with another child in school. My school library is rich with these types of stories, as are most local bookstores. **Chrysanthemum**, by Kevin Henkes addresses both the importance of names and the trials of making friends. When children write about friends, it is simply a continuation of children writing about their favorite topic – self. Who they like is all about who they are.

After the story, I announce that I am going to write about my friends. I usually focus on a name that we have already referred to during our letter/sound work. (Let's pretend the child's name is Bob.) So I begin with a pictograph (Carroll and Wilson 354) of the child in great detail, making sure to draw the child in the exact same outfit as this child is currently wearing. This maintains interest as the students attempt to guess who I am writing about. Once the children figure out the name of my subject, I decide upon a sentence. This is a very simple sentence such as "I see Bob." As before, we repeat the process of passing the boards, markers, and tissues. We also say the sentence "I see Bob," loudly like an elephant with giant clapping arms, and softly like a mouse with finger tips touching softly. Of course, we also count the words in the sentence. Then I ask, "Who remembers the first word in this sentence?" One child comes up to write the word *I*, with or without help. At this early stage, most kindergarteners prefer the lower case I, because the dot on top is so much fun. I take it! Next I remind the class that they can participate by writing the same thing on their white boards, and I give them the time to do so.

As a class we go back and read what we have already written, which is a process that will continue every single time we participate in Interactive Writing. I ask the kids to point and read. We pause after reading *I*, and I take a volunteer to come up and write, "see." Most of the time this child will only know the beginning sound, or he/she may write the letter C instead of the sound. Since this is the third day of school, and I want the kids to understand that any type of writing is writing, I take what the child offers. (Later on as we progress and feel comfortable writing, I have more specific expectations.)

Again we go back and read what we have written, pausing after whatever version of the word "see" is on the chart paper. I take a volunteer to add the word "Bob", only this time I turn the students' attention to the word "Bob" on the name/picture chart. I will call on someone to get up and point this name out to us. I slowly say the sounds of his name as the child at the chart writes "Bob" on the chart paper, and the rest of the class writes his name on their white boards. Finally, we have yet another child come up to the chart paper and place a period at the end of the sentence.

As in days one and two of Writer's Workshop, we pass the marker baskets, put away boards, and throw out tissues on the way to get journals. Most of the children write/draw about friends as I walk around and conference. A few of the children attempt to write via "saying the sounds," as in I LIKE MOM, using known letters and sounds. (Fig. 2.3) Many of the students will simply draw a picture of a friend and label it, using the name chart that is up in the classroom. To wrap up Writer's Workshop, the children come to the carpet with their journals and we will have sharing time as usual.

At this point the students have been introduced to two different tools, the "say the sounds" method, and the "looking to find a word" around the room strategy. The "say the sounds" method serves the children throughout the entire school year, although many of the students are still not able to fully utilize it this early in the school year - not yet having very many sound/letter relationships mastered.

The "looking to find a word" on a chart, Word Wall, or Word Bank strategy will also serve the children throughout the entire school year, as we create anchor charts and Word Banks to go along with various study units, and as we make use of a Word Wall for high frequency words. This early in the school year, many of the children will rely heavily on this second tool because offers them a high level of comfort.

Fig. 2.3

DAY 4, 5, 6, and 7:

Over the next four days, I continue on the topics of self and friends. I model something different each day. One day I may simply draw a couple of friends and label them; another day I may write about doing an activity with a friend, such as, "Shelby and Kim eat lunch," or, "I read with Dylan." If I introduce a Word Wall Word or add a word to a Word Bank during this time, I include that word in my writing. For example, if I introduce "like" as a Word Wall Word, my sentence would most likely be, "I like Bryce." (Fig. 2.4) During each of these sessions, I am sure to model both of the two strategies that the kids have

Fig. 2.4

learned so far. Additionally, I model all types of writing that I see in my classroom, including controlled scribbles and random strings of letters, in order to continue to validate all types of writers at this early stage.

I also like to introduce the "Spaceman" at this time. (Fig. 2.5) The "Spaceman" is just a large tongue depressor with a face drawn at the top with marker. I tell the children that the purpose of the "Spaceman" is to make sure we put a space between our words. Each day, I choose one child to come up and hold the "Spaceman" in place on the chart paper in between each word. I also give the students smaller versions of their own "Spaceman" at their tables to use in their own writing. (Fig. 2.6)

Fig. 2.5

Fig. 2.6

The "Spaceman" has always worked wonders for my students. Eventually during the school year, we give way to "finger spacing" and, finally, the kids are able to simply eyeball the proper amount of space needed between words.

DAY 8:

Thus far, I have guided the "getting ideas" component for my students by modeling my own ideas. I have modeled writing about self, writing about friends, and writing about "things I like." During this second week of school, I hand this responsibility over to the children. I wait until the children feel comfortable with pencil and paper to take this big step.

So with that in mind, on day eight, I model a story about myself. I write this as a story, introducing the concept of narrative writing—one that I can add to as the days go by. For example, I may draw a picture of myself in front of my house, and begin by writing, "One day I went outside to play in my yard. It was a sunny day." After writing this, I will model adding the extra detail of drawing a sun in the sky. Then I ask my students to begin a story in which they are the main character. (By day eight the children know that the main character is the most important person in a story because we discuss main character after each read-aloud.)

I also increase the students' writing time. While they are writing, I walk around the room and ask the students questions about their stories. During sharing time I ask two or three of the children to share their work. I encourage their listening friends to ask these young writers what they plan to add to their stories the next day.

DAY 9:

Today I continue the narrative that I began on day eight. This lets my students know they, too, may continue working on the same story over as many days as they like. I also model rereading what we have already written, before we make additions. So, I go back and read aloud the two sentences from day eight; and then ask the class to read it along with me. I remind them that my picture matches my words just like the books that we read in class. Then I add a detail to my story. "While I was playing, a little dog came up to me. I played with the dog." After I write these sentences, I will add the dog beside me in the picture I began yesterday. This way, I am modeling adding detail through both words and pictures. As discussed by Lisbeth Dixon-Krauss in **Vygotsky in the Classroom**, drawing helps students to make and demonstrate meaning, as well as helping the teacher to assess each student's literacy development (68-71).

As I walk around the room, I remind the kids to "Go back and read" what they have already written. Many children rely mainly on their pictures at this early stage, which is fine. Again, I will invite a few to share their stories, inviting questions and comments.

DAY 10:

The story from the past two days remains on the easel so I can continue to work on the same piece. Of course, rereading the previous writing takes place before adding to my story each day. On day ten I might add something like: "I gave the dog a bowl of food and a bowl of water." Again I will add this detail to my drawing.

Usually there are a few kids who do not wish to return to their stories. While most are excited to continue on their story, a few are not. Those who do not wish to return to their story are now out of their comfort zone. I find that these kids generally want to return to practicing their name, or their friends' names, or even labeling pictures. All of this is fine. I simply recognize that my students are at different stages in their level of comfort, as well as on different levels of development. As long as they are happy "writing," I am happy. Writing as an ongoing process takes place throughout the entire school year, so these children can progress as they become ready.

Over the next few days, I continue to model by adding to the same story until I bring it to an end on day twelve. I realize that my students are each working at their own developmental level on day twelve. Some of the children will be developing new ideas. Many children will be bringing their narratives to a close and will be ready to begin publishing. I want to model the beginning of publishing, so I introduce this concept on day thirteen.

DAY 13:

As a class we will reread the entire story, which has now reached a conclusion. I tell the class that I really like this story. "I am very proud of my story. I wonder if I can do anything that would make my story even better." If a child has a suggestion of a detail I could add, I take that suggestion and immediately add it to my story. I may have to write this suggestion down the side of the page, add a caret (ˇ), or even use a "spider leg," which is a thin strip of paper that is attached to a piece of writing so that an additional sentence can be added. This is the beginning of revision. I do not revise any more at this early stage in the year. I simply want to introduce the concept. Next, I invite the young writers to return to their stories. They may wish to read their stories to a friend and ask for suggestions, or they may wish to work alone. Some may make additions, and some may not. (Figure 2.7)

Fig. 2.7

DAY 14:

Today I tell my class that I want to share my story with someone else, perhaps the principal or another teacher. "I am going to write this story on some really special paper (not chart size) so that I can present it to someone else." I write my story on white typing paper in my very best writing and I include a picture. Some teachers type a child's story for them if desired. Some children simply want to edit their original piece, as recreating a work can seem overwhelming. Again, this is extremely early in the school year, and I am introducing a concept to my kids that we will visit and revisit many times during the year.

During publishing time, the kids work within their own sphere of comfort and development. During sharing time today, I am one of the people that will share with the class.

DAY 15:

On day fifteen, I place my story into a construction paper cover during the modeling portion of our Writer's Workshop. I ask the class to come along with me as I present my story to my special person. I especially like to take my class to the principal, if he/she is available. It is exciting for the class to watch as their teacher presents this story as a gift. I always read my story aloud to the special person because I will someday want my kids to do the same. (At Northwood Hills Elementary School, the entire office staff is wonderful about allowing the students to come in and read their works, often rewarding the young authors with a nice note.)

Upon return to the classroom, I begin modeling the beginning of a new story…and the process continues.

We continue Writer's Workshop daily, making sure to follow the same routines and procedures until my children fully understand my plan for each day's process. Later in the year I make changes as needed, but it is imperative to start off using a routine that my kids can walk through daily.

Possible goals for future Kindergarten Writer's Workshops:
- demonstrating how to choose a topic to write about (and creating a topic list)
- teaching children to raise their hands if they need a conference
- encouraging students to go back and reread what they have already written
- modeling helpful questions and comments for sharing time
- using pictures as prewriting plans
- saying words slowly to listen for the sounds they make – ongoing
- using a word wall for high frequency words or an anchor chart/a word bank for important words in a particular theme or an academic subject - ongoing
- introducing a "draft book" or "author's book"
- adding more to what has already been written
- simple drafting or revising, such as giving details about a setting, or additional information about characters
- simple editing, such as spaces between words, writing left to right, punctuation
- writing a story with a beginning, middle, and end
- choosing a new idea to write about

This is by no means a complete list of goals for all Writer's Workshop mini-lessons, nor should it be. My students' writing always leads me into creating needed goals for my budding writers. If I invest in spending time conferencing with students daily, they will show me where to lead them.

Prewriting

Writing Roulette

Writing Roulette is a prewriting strategy, explained in *Acts of Teaching*, by Carroll and Wilson. Actually a collaborative narrative, one person begins writing a story, then passes this beginning on to the next person, who reads the beginning and adds to it, then passes the story on to the next person who does the same. This process continues until each participant in the small group has had an opportunity to contribute to the story. The last person in the group wraps the story up with a conclusion.

Writing Roulette is really fun with kindergarteners. They are so funny and creative. We like to sit around one table together as a small group. If the kids have been doing Interactive Writing, the concept of Writing Roulette makes sense to them. They are used to sharing ideas and having one idea align with the next idea, (the beginning of coherence and organization) even if that idea belongs to someone else. I usually write the first sentence, just to get the ball rolling. At this age I invite each child to add one sentence. This is not because they wouldn't be able to write more—some would add an entire page! I do this to maintain attention span. It is easier to wait for "your turn"… if it won't be too terribly long. I also encourage the students to talk and share what they wrote as they are passing. Each child usually reads his or her sentence aloud to the entire group, which is about four or six children. This helps maintain attention on the task, and better ideas surface. Additionally, all the children know the direction of passing before we begin. I realize it may sound trivial to mention the importance of passing, but I do not want anything to distract from the topic and task. The last child in the circle knows that he or she needs to wrap up the story if possible. The two stories below are examples of groups experiencing Writing Roulette for the first time.

The first sample (Fig. 3.1) was written a group of six kindergartens and me. The story reads:

> *One day I saw a dog. He was brown. A cat came along.*
> *the dog ate the cat. the dog throo up. the cat popt out uv*
> *his mouth.*

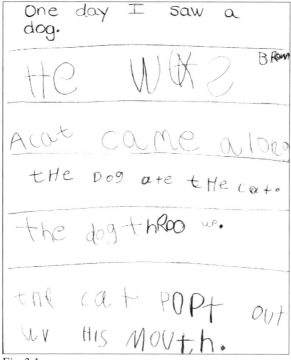

Fig. 3.1

I ask all the children to sign their names at the bottom of the story.

The second sample was written by a group of five kindergarteners and me. The story reads:

> On a dark night, I heard footsteps. I thot it was a monster.
> But it was my cat. the cat sed meow. He was hungry.

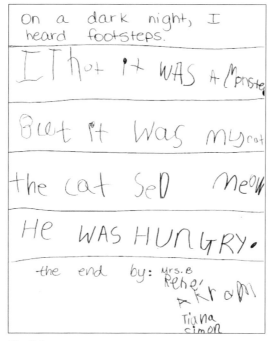

Fig. 3.2

This is a great prewriting tool for young ones when they get stuck for ideas. Writing Roulette gets the "mental ball rolling" for my kindergarteners. If they like, they can take the short story they have worked on with their group and expand it into a more detailed narrative, adding characters and events. Or, they may just use an idea brought out during this process and turn that idea into an entirely new piece. I tend to introduce Writing Roulette during the second semester of kindergarten. By this time, not only are the students more experienced writers, but they also are better at working in a collaborative group. It is important to choose groups carefully for the first attempt at Writing Roulette.   There is always a danger of domination by one child who may attempt to tell the other students what to write during their turn in order to control the outcome of the story. This is another reason that I like to be a member of each group myself. When I explained this process at a Abydos Learning Institute this past summer, one of the participants asked a very good question. She wondered what the rest of my twenty-two students were doing while I participated in a session of Writing Roulette with one small group. In my classroom, the remainder of the class participates in centers when I facilitate a small group writing strategy. This way I am able to give my small group my undivided attention, and I can be a true participant.

It is fun to ask each group if they would like to share their stories with the entire class. This can be done by asking the members of each group to read their pieces aloud, or by photocopying the stories on a transparency. This later procedure enables the entire class to read along. Presto—we have a piece for shared reading! These stories are added to a center for enjoyment by all the children.

Blueprinting

Blueprinting is a fun prewriting activity explained in **Acts of Teaching** (72). Kindergarteners love to express themselves, and this is the perfect opportunity for them to do so. I always introduce Blueprinting to my students in a small group setting. The small group offers the opportunity for talking and sharing ideas. I encourage the children to talk during the entire process of Blueprinting. As evidenced in the video, this talking allows the children and me to share and glean ideas from one another. In so doing, we form a group understanding of the process of Blueprinting and what it entails.

We begin at the horseshoe table in a small group of four or five children and me. I give each of the students a large piece of construction paper that they fold into a gate fold. Each outside edge of the paper is folded inward, to where they meet in the middle. This creates the look of two doors opening up. I like this fold because many of my students live in apartments, and this fold allows the child to create either an apartment or a house. We begin with our homes closed.

I invite the students to decorate this closed form to look like the outside of their own homes. I do this by using my own home as an example. I talk as I draw the roof, windows, door, and so on. This lets the students know that they can talk as they work. Rather than telling my kids to label each item, I point out that I am labeling each part of my own home. We continue to discuss what each person is adding to the outside of each home. As we reach the point that we are ready to begin work in the inside of our homes, I tell the students that I am going to open my house and begin to "show" the rooms that are inside. I try to choose my words carefully so that each child feels comfortable to create his or her own home in a way that is not controlled by me. This is difficult because I must constantly be aware of my words.

For example, once when one of my students did not draw a bed, it would have been easy for me to ask, "Where is the bed?" I am so glad I did not ask this question. As she writes and talks, I discover that she, her mother, and her grandmother, all sleep on the floor of their apartment. Because I have not made her uncomfortable, she happily tells me all about the people lying together on the floor of her apartment.

Fig. 3.3

In fact, all of the children chatter excitedly about the rooms and the inside of their homes. I begin to label the rooms of my own home, hoping the kids will notice. One of them does, and our discussions continue. I make sure I give time and attention to each child. Everyone has a time to share with the group.

Fig. 3.4

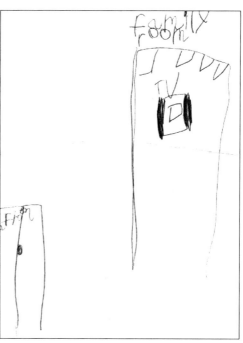

Fig. 3.5

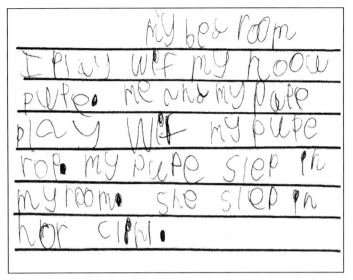

Fig. 3.6

When I am satisfied that the children have had ample time to complete their Blueprints, I pass out a second piece of paper. I offer my kids lined paper, but some teachers prefer unlined. At this point, I ask my students to choose a favorite room they wish to write about. I ask them to tell us why they like their special room and what they enjoy doing in it. As usual, we talk as we write. "Leighton, tell us about your favorite room." She thinks for a moment before responding, "I really like my bedroom the most because of my new puppy. She sleeps in my room in her kennel." The kids continue to share their ideas. I hear one child making the sounds of the letters as he writes the words. I write as well. Upon completion, each child takes a turn reading aloud. We make comments on the pieces we hear. I usually end by reading my piece. Below is an example of a piece of writing by one of the students that originated from the Blueprinting strategy (Figs. 3.3-3.6).

Pentad

The Pentad is a prewriting strategy laid out by Carroll and Wilson in *Acts of Teaching* (76). The Pentad is a wonderful prewriting tool because it can be used with both fiction and nonfiction writing. I find this strategy easiest to introduce to my students after a read-aloud.

During the month of February, I read the story, *Clifford's First Valentines' Day*. I have a discussion with my students about the events in this story. To help retain the facts of the story, we create a short retelling using Interactive Writing. (For more information on retelling with primary students, see *Read and Retell, A Strategy for the Whole Language/Natural Learning Classroom* by Cambourne and Brown).

I only make use of this short retelling (Fig. 3.7) the first time I introduce the Pentad, and it is strictly used as an aid in the creation of the Pentad. I want the students to be able to recall the events of the story with ease this very first time.

Fig. 3.7

We began the Pentad by creating the graphic organizer (star) on a large piece of chart paper. Instead of using Burke's terms, "Action, Actor, Scene, Purpose and Agency," I use more age appropriate terms. I tell the children that we are going to record important facts from our story. In front of the children, I write the questions:

Who?
When?
Where?
What?
How?   and
Why?

I call on volunteers to come up to the chart to write the names of the main characters of the Clifford story as the rest of the class writes along on their white boards. This is placed under the point of the star entitled "Who?" We also answer the questions about the setting of the story in the same manner, which is placed under the "When? Where?" point of the star. When we approach the point of the star that asks "What?" I know that my children will require some clarification. I explain that in this section, we will write about "what happened" in the story. Often this is the problem, or the climax of the story. With this understanding established, I ask for a volunteer to come up with a sentence letting us know "what happened." This question is answered with ease, and the sentence is written Interactively. Now that we have established "What?" it is quite simple for the children to come up with the answers to both the "How?" and the "Why" sections of the star. Once the Pentad is complete, we review all of our answers, and check them by referring back to the book. (Fig. 3.8)

On the very same day that I introduce the Pentad during the read-aloud, I ask the children to make use of this graphic organizer independently. This occurs during Independent Reading Time, which we call "book boxes," because the children have a collection of books, kept in a plastic box, on their particular reading level (and above) that they choose from freely. I ask the children to select a favorite book from their book box. I provide them with a copy of a personal Pentad and ask

Fig. 3.8

them to complete this Pentad using their chosen text. The children enjoy this activity when they are given the freedom to explore the Pentad alongside of a book they enjoy.

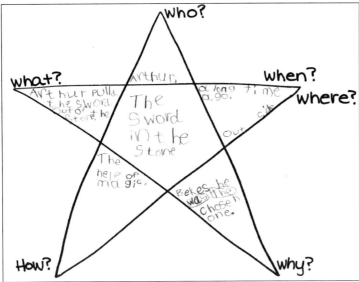

One student chose to use an old, but well loved fictional tale, *The Sword in the Stone*. (Fig. 3.9)

Fig. 3.9

Another child, using the exact same book box, chose a non-fiction book, *Discovery Teams*. (Fig. 3.10)

I review the Pentads created by my students to determine the level of understanding of each student. Once it is evident that my children have mastered the concept of the Pentad (at a kindergarten

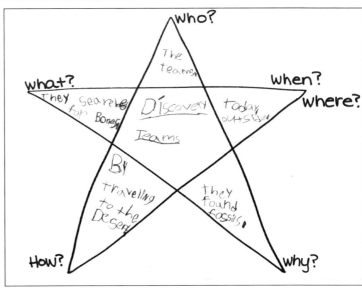

Fig. 3.10

level, of course), I invite them to create their own Pentad to use as a graphic organizer when writing their own drafts.

The Pentad is wonderful resource for the child who is full of many great ideas, but loses focus while writing. The Pentad brings the child back to their original thought process, which helps when a child trails off in the middle of a great story, suddenly writing about something that has nothing to do with the original idea. This can happen often with young writers, and it is so nice to have that Pentad right next to the student to refer to when I want to bring a student back to focus on the piece. The Pentad also helps the teacher be more of a facilitator, and less of a dictator. As a teacher with pretty high expectations, I am personally grateful for the Pentad. Sometimes my students need a break from me looking over their shoulder all the time. The Pentad also gives me the confidence to know that my students are writing with a purpose, and I can back off and allow my young writers some independence.

The Pentad here features the young author (Blair) and two of his friends as the main characters. (Fig. 3.11) The Setting occurs in the daytime in a creek. I love that his story takes place in a creek; I can only imagine that this young man has an exact creek in mind.

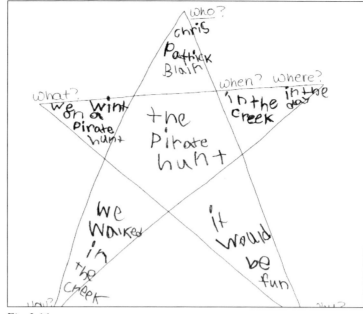
Fig. 3.11

His story remains true to his Pentad. (Fig. 3.12) Blair's story reads:

The Pirate Hunt

   Three friends named Chris Patrick and Blair went in the creek. It was fun. We had eye patches. It was fun jumping from rock to rock. Beside the rock there was a treasure of Bamboo. We made spears with the Bamboo. The end

   The Pentad is a graphic organizer that truly helps students gain a higher level

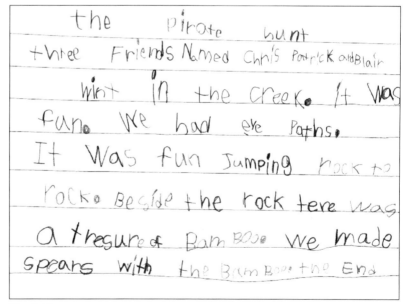
Fig. 3.12

of comprehension in their reading, as well as being an excellent tool for young writers. It enables young students to take part in the beginning of literary analysis, helping them to view a story from different aspects. Knowing how to use a Pentad will serve my students for the rest of their academic careers. The older the child becomes, the more complex the Pentad can become to accommodate that child. The Pentad offers clarity, organization, and confidence. Not only can my students appreciate these gifts, I am sincerely grateful for them as a teacher.

4 Family Writing

What gets kindergarten kids writing early in the year?   Family

Every kindergarten teacher knows getting young children to take their first baby steps into becoming writers is not easy. Writing is a risk, and little ones do not always warm up to the idea of taking such a risk.

So, I begin with topics that children feel comfortable with—topics that they have a great deal of knowledge about. Five year olds, especially in September when many of them are still be longing for Mommy, love the idea of writing about family. They are experts on this topic - and we all love to share when we are experts. And, as research shows us, children are only able to write about topics on which they have knowledge and experience. As Dorn and Soffos state in *Scaffolding Young Writers*, "The first step, that of coming up with an idea, is based on our experiences and knowledge-in other words, our thoughts" (2).

There are a great many books that help foster the belief that each child is an expert in the field of family; and further more, that others are greatly interested in this topic as well. This instills the notion that "other people will care about my writing."

The list is endless, but a few good books about family include:

In the Rain with Baby Duck	Amy Hest
Mama Zooms	Jane Cowen-Fletcher
Just Grandpa and Me	Mercer Mayer
The Baby Sister	Tomie dePaola
Mama Provi and the Pot of Rice	Sylvia Rosa-Casanova
The Seven Silly Eaters	Marla Frazee
What Mommies Do Best	Laura Numeroff
What Daddies Do Best	Laura Numeroff
One of Three	Angela Johnson
When I am Old with You	Angela Johnson
A Chair for my Mother	Vera B. Williams
Guess How much I Love You	Sam McBratney
Brothers and Sisters	Ellen B Senisi
When Mama Comes Home Tonight	Eileen Spinelli

Kim Dumaine

Family is a topic that all students have experienced. They find comfort in being able to "write what they know." Family is a great topic to use early on when I wish to establish a Writer's Workshop climate in my classroom. I like to use family as a topic when I am teaching writing behavior and procedures because instilling rules can be threatening to some youngsters. This can be balanced by the comforting thoughts of family members.

My goal for this particular session of Writer's Workshop, as evidenced in the video, is simply to center on procedures. I want each child to be fully aware of acceptable behaviors during writer's workshop. This is essential at the kindergarten level. My expectations for behaviors are obvious in this video. I do want to make note that this does not occur automatically. We are actually still in the process of mastering expectations during the time this video was taken. The best advice I can offer is that the teacher must decide what Writer's Workshop will look like in his/her classroom. Then model, model, model, and practice, practice, practice (with consistency) what those behaviors should look like. Because I have a tiny classroom, and it always has twenty-two kids, I run a pretty tight ship. This approach may not work for everyone.

I want the students to offer up ideas when we begin to write as a class. In the following example, two sentences have been built so far. Both of these were "thought up" by a student in the class. We then add the sentences to the story through Interactive Writing. In this example (Fig 4.1), students wrote:

Mi mom is great.
Mom can bak cukees.

Fig. 3.12

Since my goal for this session is to teach behaviors, I am not worried about the spelling. Cunningham and Allington present this idea in **Classrooms That Work** (91). Some people believe that this is a mistake—that any type of modeling (and this is modeling) should make use of proper spelling. The belief is that it is perfectly fine for individual students to spell phonetically in their own individual writing, but modeled writing should always be correct. I adhere to this philosophy myself. But like any rule, I also believe there are times when rules need to be suspended. For further reading on modeling in the kindergarten classroom, I suggest **....And with a Light Touch** by Carol Avery, **Apprenticeship in Literacy** by Dorn, French, and Jones, and **Interactive Writing** by McCarrier, Pinnell and Fountas.

Now early to mid September, I am fully aware that every single student does not have the letter/sound relationship mastered. And I certainly know that none of my students have any of the more difficult laws of spelling under their belts. For example, none of my children are aware that "my" is spelled M Y, so when M I is offered, I take it with a smile on my face. Secretly, I know that "my" will soon be a Word Wall Word, so this experience will later aid me with the teaching of the word "my" with its unusual spelling, which would not make sense at this point.

At the moment I am not teaching Word Wall Words or spelling. I am teaching behaviors, and that is our main focus. And I know that soon I will be able to hold the children accountable for known words, such as Word Wall words. Knowing myself well and having a plan, helps a great deal with these issues.

I also expect that the child who is **not** coming up to the chart to write a word will be engaged in writing the same word on his/her white board. The children control their markers to make certain that the ONLY writing taking place occurs on the white boards. I check to ensure that this is happening regularly. (I am trying to stop certain habits before they begin, such as using a marker to mark on the carpet or another child's clothing.) Here are two examples (Figs. 4.2 & 4.3) which show this behavior.

In Fig. 4.2 the child in the lower left corner is marking the capret. In 4.3, the child has just marked her t-shirt.

Fig. 4.2

Fig. 4.3

The passing out and picking up of boards, markers, and tissues requires a great deal of practice during the first two weeks of school; after that it becomes second nature. The children also need to know that independent writing time is exactly that, and not a time to get up, talk to a friend, or play in centers. Insisting upon this behavior will have big payoffs later.

The students know that I am coming around to conference with them, and that they may need to be patient if I am busy. I tell then to "keep writing until I get there."

It is also important for the children to be good listeners during "share time." It may seem difficult to ensure this behavior at first, but later, I am always so happy that I took the time to teach this procedure. In the beginning of the year, I save my sanity by allowing only two or three young writers to share after each workshop.

Here is a series of students' samples about their families:

Jonathan is a big fan of writing about *family*. His first sample in September simple states:

Dad can cook

Fig. 4.4

Leighton states the obvious:

My mom is beautiful.

Fig. 4.5

Cale states (Fig. 4.6):

Mommy bakes cookies.

Fig. 4.6

Katherine is writing mainly with beginning sounds (Fig. 4.7), although she catches a few others in:

My dad loves me.

Fig. 4.7

In Tiana's first sample, I learn that her mom is a princess (Fig. 4.8), and in her second sample (Fig. 4.9), I read:

My dad can race with me.

Fig. 4.8

Fig. 4.9

Pierce uses FAMILY as his inspiration for four days:

I like my brother to swim, falls below the word Family and appears above the list of his family member's names.

Fig. 4.10

My mom can play board games. (Fig. 4.11)

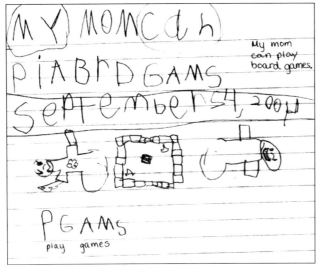

Fig. 4.11

I like my mom. I like my dad. I like me. I like my daddy with me. I like my mom to eat with me. (Fig. 4.12)

Fig. 4.12

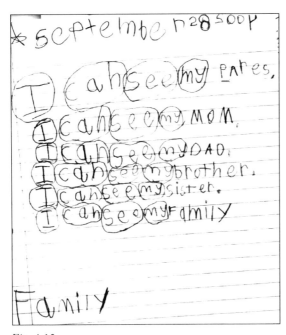

I can see my parents. I can see my mom. I can see my dad. I can see my brother. I can see my sister. I can see my family. Family (Fig. 4.13)

Fig. 4.13

The children have circled certain words in some of their writing. These circles also appear on the class chart of Interactive Writing. The words circled are our current Word Wall Words. I encourage students to notice Word Wall Words in their own writing by circling them. This practice is fun for the kids and gets results.

It helps to note that we have a family tree poster on the wall for a reference, which displays names for family members, such as Mom, Dad, Brother, and Sister. This serves as a word bank for those students wishing to use it.

Introducing the idea of writing about family greatly reduces youngsters' fears about writing. It is a subject they will return to often, and it is a subject about which each student has some prior knowledge. Introducing this subject early in the school year significantly reduces the age old, "I can't think of anything to write about."

Finally, I decide upon a routine for putting writing away. Once I find a system that works, I stick to it. I only allow seven students at a time to put their writing away, as all the "Writer's Workshop Boxes" are kept in the same area; I do not want a traffic jam. Making decisions about my own classroom routines and sticking to them is imperative to my sanity and the success of my students. It seems overwhelming in the beginning, but I always like to remember: "More work now means less work later!"

At the end of our Family Unit, I assign a project to be completed at home. Every child constructs a Family Tree of his or her own, which includes photos or drawings of the family. Each child uses this "tree" to introduce the class to each family member. Upon completion of each presentation, we display each Family Tree in the hall (Fig. 4.14). This instills pride in my students and sets up a practice that will take place often during the school year. I want my students to be very comfortable presenting their work aloud and having it on display, as this will be a constant practice in Writer's Workshop as part of the publishing process.

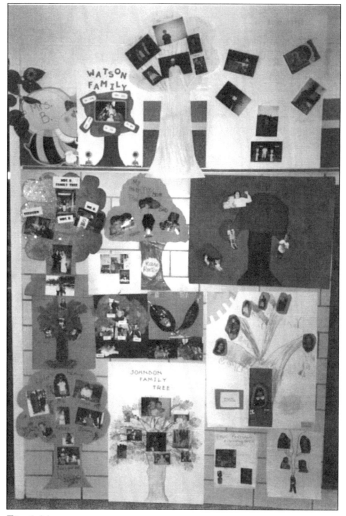

Fig. 4.14

5. Responding to Literature

Fairy Tales and Nursery Rhymes

serve as wonderful tools to encourage kindergarteners to respond to literature, especially early in the school year when they are not experienced writers. Most kindergarteners are somewhat familiar with most fairy tales, even if it is only through the Disney movies. The Fairy Tale unit usually begins late September or early October. By then most of the children have command of the letter/sound relationship, and those who are not completely there yet have enough letters and sounds in their repertoire to be able to participate actively in class sessions of Interactive Writing.

We study fairy tales and nursery rhymes for almost an entire month. As a class, we respond to the literature in some written form. For the first week of this unit, I choose most of the books that we respond to. By the second week, the children are beginning to bring in their own fairy tales and nursery rhymes. Our classroom is overflowing with both modern day and classic versions of the children's favorites from home, my own books, and stories checked out from the school library. The children peruse these stories during "free reading" time. They also take the books with them to the tables during writing time. I want the children to have ample opportunity to explore and become familiar with these stories, so that they will be confident in their written responses.

After studying a few different versions of ***Jack and the Beanstalk,*** we offered Jack some advice for making better choices. (Many fun ideas for responding to fairy tales can be found in the book *Interactive Writing*, by McCarrier, Pinnell and Fountas.)

Advice to Jack

Listen to your mom.
Get muney four the cow.
Stop stealing.

Fig. 5.1

This chart (Fig. 5.1) was created as an entire class using Interactive Writing. This serves as an early prewriting activity because it models the thinking involved in responding to literature. Students are able to discuss ideas with peers during this process. In this way, they are able to learn from one another.

Cinderella offers us the opportunity to practice pulling key events from a story, as a response to hearing it read aloud. I ask for a child from the class to offer up a sentence telling us what happened in the Beginning of the story, which we write interactively. I ask if someone else can come up with an idea telling what happened in the Middle of the story. Someone raises their hand and shares their idea, which we then add to the chart. As we get ready for the sentence that describes the End of the story, several hands are up, so we are able to hear many suggestions. As a class we agree on the sentence we feel best describes the End and record it interactively.

Cinderella

B   they found out about the ball.

M   She did not have time to make her dress.

E   the fairy came and made her dress and she got marred.

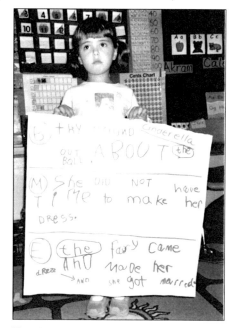

Fig. 5.2

As a class, we also gave *Humpty Dumpty* some ideas to avoid cracking:

*Carry bandaids
never sit on a wall.
Be careful.*

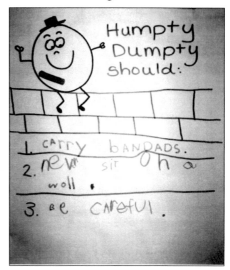

Fig. 5.2

We used **Little Red Riding Hood** to practice an early version of Blueprinting, as found in **Acts of Teaching,** by Carroll and Wilson(72). After reading this story, I invite the children to talk about the story as a class. We discuss the characters in the story, the setting, and the events. We decide to create a collage as a response to the story. "This will help us remember the important ideas from this story," I tell the kids. Kindergarteners love to express themselves through art, so this idea is appealing to the entire class. Each student participated in adding something to the collage. Some came right up to the chart and used markers on it; others chose to create a part of the story at their tables with their own supplies, to later be placed on the collage we are creating. This activity is a big winner with the kids because they see instant results.

Fig. 5.3

On the last day of studying fairy tales and nursery rhymes, everyone in the class (Fig. 5.4) comes to school dressed as their favorite character and gives on oral report (Fig. 5.5 & 5.6).

Fig. 5.4

Karlee
Book
Report

Fig. 5.2

Promesa
Book
Report

Fig. 5.2

Some of the oral reports are extremely elaborate, for example one young man did an entire retelling of **Pinocchio**, complete with song and dance. Still other children simply state the name of their character along with the name of the actual fairy tale. All reports are greeted with cheers from peers and are listened to with great interest. This day gives purpose to all the prewriting activities previously explained. This day also gives meaning to all of the fairy tales we have studied. And it especially gives meaning to all the individual writing in response to fairy tales that the children have done in their journals.

Fig. 5.8

Finally, we write a "Modern Fairy Tale." This is done as a whole class, using Interactive Writing. It includes modern a day setting, along with characters from our classroom:

*Once upon a time there was a little girl named Kate. She was trapped in a **Pizza Hut** * by a monster. Rene gave the monster some Oreos. The monster left the Pizza Hut. Akram took Kate and ran away.*

* Instead of writing **Pizza Hut** here, we cut the label off of a pizza box and glued it into the story.

As it is fairly early in the school year, most of the children do not totally understand concepts of print, as they will later on in the year. They all, however, understand that what they have to say is important and worth reading. They also understand how to use constructed, or phonetic spelling, to convey a message. This is due do the continued use of Interactive Writing as a prewriting strategy during writer's workshop. Each day the slow sounding out of words to identify sounds during Interactive Writing increases each students' ability to apply this knowledge to their own individual writing.

Fig. 5.9

I have included some individual responses to fairy tales that students have recorded in their journals.

Pierce responds (Fig. 5.10) to **Jack and the Beanstalk** by first writing the words *Jack"* and *Giant."*

Then he writes,

I hope Jack is better in the next story.

He draws the beans that Jack *should* have refused to trade, and writes the word,"

NO.

Fig. 5.10

Pierce also responds to **Humpty Dumpty** with a retelling (Fig. 5.11) with a happy ending.

Humpty Dumpty had a great fall. All the kings horse's and king's men **could** *put Humpty back together.*

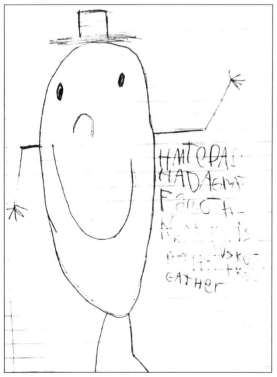

Fig. 5.11

After reading **Sleeping Beauty**, Pierce writes (Fig. 5.12),

I like castles especially the top room.

Fig. 5.12

Fig. 5.13

Simon responds (Fig. 5.13) to **The Three Pigs** by writing,

I am a three little pig.

He responds (Fig. 5.14) to **Jack and the Beanstalk** with sympathy for the cow:

I like bull cow.

I ask Simon, "What does your cow say?"

He adds,

Moo.

Fig. 5.14

Fig. 5.15

Cale responds (Fig. 5.15) to **Humpty Dumpty** simply,

I like Humpty Dumpty.

He changes (Fig. 5.16) *The Old Woman Who Lived in a Shoe* into

The little boy in a shoe" and adds the word "laces.

Fig. 5.16

Fig. 5.17

He also responds (Fig. 5.17) to *Little Red Riding Hood* with his depiction of "Little Red Riding."

The caption reads,

litdl red riding.

During sharing time, the students read their works to any friend they choose, me, or even the entire class if they like.

These children are self-confident writers even during the first week of October. They are allowed freedom within a structure. Yes, Writer's Workshop is structured freedom. However, since the kids are able to write as much or as little as they would like and are allowed to write about whatever they like, they are given the freedom needed to express themselves as a writer in a safe setting. This encourages the children to take risks as writers. Risks mean growth. Growth brings more confidence. And so the cycle continues and gains strength. Even at such an early date in the school year, a kindergarten classroom can be taken through the process of writing. As a writing teacher, I must believe in my students and their abilities. I expect a great deal of my young writers, and they never let me down.

6 Response to an Author

This exercise also takes place in early in the school year—usually in late October or early November. I like to introduce the concept of voice early on when the children are just beginning to perceive themselves as writers. We discuss that when we use voice in writing, it is easy to know "who is doing the talking" by what they are saying, and how they are saying it. **Green Eggs and Ham** is a wonderful example of two characters with completely different voices.

I build excitement by introducing the well-loved children's book by Dr. Seuss, whom all the students know well and love. I present the story of **Green Eggs and Ham** through a read aloud, followed by the video **Green Eggs and Ham**. We stop occasionally throughout the story to look at the voice of the two characters. Each character in this story has an obvious voice. One is extremely excited, and the other is reserved. We use the video to help us discover the voice of each character in the story.

As a class we create instructions for cooking green eggs and ham, which we actually follow as we cook them, so that we could taste green eggs and ham for ourselves. Each sentence was "thought up" by a student in the classroom. If we all come to agreement that we like this sentence, we add it through the use of Interactive Writing. Using this format, every child in the room takes part in or contributes to the entire piece, even if they only come up to add a period at the end of a sentence. This helps in the fostering of a "writing community" in which every child sees every peer as a writer and cohort. Our instructions (Fig. 6.1) for making green eggs and ham read:

green eggs and ham
Put eggs in a bowl.
Add the Ham. Add
green food coloring.
Mix it up. Last you
cook it.
eat it.
the end

Fig. 6.1

At this point we cook and eat the eggs and ham. I make sure to review the reason for writing the directions; so that we can follow them. I remind the kids of this fact so that they do not get confused and think that I want them to create a How-To piece.

I invite the kids to get out their journals and respond to Dr. Seuss, attempting to show their own **voice.** We break into groups and discuss individual ideas for responses. I walk around and drop in on the groups, listening to discover whether I need to lead the discussion toward responding to the story with one of my own suggestions, or simply let the kids know that they are on the right track. Most of the students feel the strong need to tell Dr. Seuss what they think of the green eggs and ham, with the exception of Cale, (Fig. 6.2) who takes it upon himself to create a T-chart and interview friends in the room for their opinions.

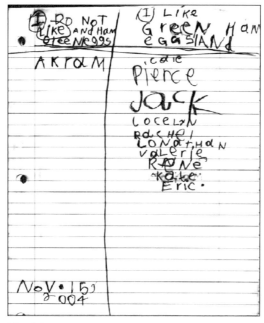

Fig. 6.1

Responding to Literature

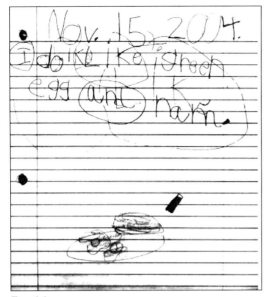

Fig. 6.3

Katherine writes (Fig. 6.4):

I do like my green eggs and ham. Rachel and me could eat green eggs and ham.

Fig. 5.15

Kate simply writes (Fig. 6.3):

I do like green eggs and ham, along with a drawing.

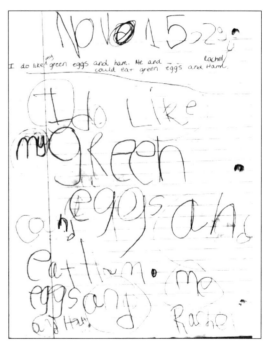

Fig. 6.4

Pierce creates a very artistic version of various sentences twisted together (Fig. 6.5), including:

The eggs are goodest, I really love green eggs, that is yum, really yum, and many more.

Luckily he changes to a different color crayon for each sentence.

Rene writes (Fig. 6.6):

I like it. YUM. I want more.

Fig. 6.6

Tiana attempts (Fig. 6.7) to use the style of the author:

I like green eggs and ham. I do in the dark.

Fig. 6.7

Yitzi's feelings (Fig. 6.8) are visibly strong:

I do NOT like green eggs and ham.

Notice the drawing with the frown included.

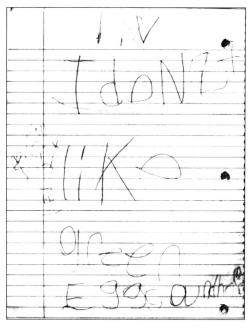

Fig. 6.8

This is our first attempt to examine **voice** as a minilesson. Not all of the children let their voice come through as strongly as I might like, but I try to remember this is an introduction to **voice,** and the children were successful in responding to the text and the activity. And, after all, it is only about the sixth week of school.

Finally, the kids get back into groups by sitting in small circles on the floor throughout the room, so that they can share their writing with one another, inviting questions and comments.

The "question and comments" part of sharing has been modeled since the first day of school. Each child knows to quietly show "attentive listening" as the author is sharing, then raise a hand if a question or comment comes to mind. The author then calls on a peer with a raised hand. Each author is allowed two questions or comments from fellow students. This is a hard and fast rule in my classroom. It is important to allow for the maximum amount of sharing.

During whole group sharing in several previous writer's workshops, I have modeled appropriate "questions and comments" to ensure that these sharing times will be worthwhile. If this part of sharing is not modeled, every child who raises a hand will say: "I like your writing." This is okay for the first week of school, but I really want the kids to put some thought behind their questions and comments, so that both author and listeners may glean ideas for the future from this experience.

An appropriate comment might be: "I heard your voice when you said YUM really loud." An appropriate question might be: "Why did you include Rachel in your story?" (This is actually a popular question.) The response is usually something like, "Because she is sweet." As time progresses I will model using greater detail during "questions and comments."

Overall I am pleased not only with the students' writing, but also with the behaviors and procedures that they are beginning to master. These behaviors are essential in creating a successful climate during writer's workshop. Without them writer's workshop would be a behavior management nightmare for the rest of the year. And my motto in all things kindergarten has always been: *"More work now means less work later!"*

Nothing is more wonderful than being able to sit back and observe during second semester as the children begin to take over and writer's workshop can run itself. This is when I get to become the facilitator rather than the teacher. And I get to spend longer with each child during conferencing because I am not so badly needed by every single student. They have become independent learners.

At this time during the school year, however, my students need me to be by their sides as much as possible. I move quickly through the classroom as they write, helping certain children to "say the sounds slowly" as they write, or helping certain others to "think about what they want to say" before they begin writing. It is vitally important that my students master the *behaviors* of a young writer during writer's workshop as well. I continually remind them to "raise their hand for a conference" or to "go back and read" what they have written. As a kindergarten teacher, I know I will be extremely busy helping the students during these early months of school. I also know that my investment will pay off soon.

7 How-to Writing

As a teacher of very young children, I see the value of How-To writing. One benefit is that it helps the children to think in a sequential order as they write. This aids all of their writing. Even narratives must follow a logical sequential order, and practicing How-To writing strengthens this important skill. This ability to think and write in a sequential order also benefits my students in other subject areas, such as math and science. I usually begin teaching the concept of How-To writing sometime in November, and revisit it several times during the school year.

I begin by reading the book *Pizza*, by Saturino Romay. I ask the students to notice that this book is different from a regular storybook. "This book gives us directions and tells us how to do something. (Fig. 7.1) If we follow the directions given in this book, we can make pizza." As a class we discuss the vocabulary we might need to help us remember to put things in the correct order. Words such as *First, Next, Then, Last,* and *Now,* are listed and hung up in the classroom for future reference. These ordinal words serve the students as early organizational tools. I do not require the students to use these words in their individual writing, but they are available to the children.

As a class we decide to write our own directions for making a pizza, and then follow them. (Fig. 7.2) For

Fig. 7.1

Fig. 7.2

prewriting, we use Interactive Writing to create these directions on chart paper. This takes about three sessions of Interactive Writing. I also invite children to come up and circle Word Wall words and underline the ordinal words, such as *First, Next, Then, and Last*. We read these directions several times during Shared Reading. As promised, we follow the directions and make individual pizzas (Fig. 7.3) in order to give further value to writing our first How-To. Children write their own versions in their journals or on paper provided.

Fig. 7.3

Kim Dumaine

This sample does not employ these sequential words; but, Tianna is able to express her point well, and even uses a touch of voice in her piece, which rings of a narrative:

How To Make Pizza
My mom helps me make pizza.
We get dough. We get sauce.
We get cheese. We cook it. YUM

This piece gives clear instruction while maintaining the writing style of the author.

From there I invite the students to create their own individual How-To pieces that can be shared with the rest of the class. The children write up directions for personal favorite dishes. One writes out the instructions for making salad, while another explains the art of taco making, and a third gives directions for baking a cake. It is during this second round of How-To writing

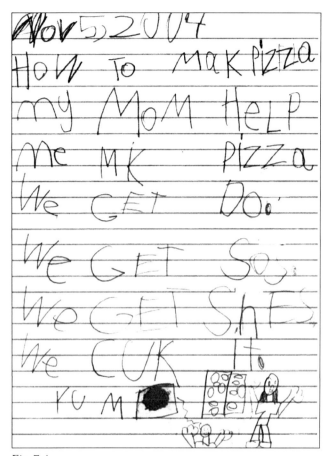

Fig. 7.4

that I notice the writing of a small number of my students is dangerously close to sounding formulaic. This can happen sometimes when children loose interest in their writing- when writing becomes an assignment, and no longer a personal joy. This is a learning experience for me. I know that I need to give my children greater freedom to express themselves more freely and creatively. I am thankful for this information, and will make use of it promptly in class discussions and individual conferences.

Weeks later, I attempt to revisit the How -To with a topic that is less concrete, hoping for more individualism. So we write about getting ready for school in the morning. This seems like a great idea. After all, no two children have the exact same morning routine. As a class we discuss the importance of creating a unique piece that is all about self. But the result is the same. Very little self.

Now I realize the problem is actually me. I am being the controlling teacher, albeit unwittingly. Yes, we tried How -To writing another way, but who made the assignment? I took the power away from my students when I *told* them what to write about. It is not like me to give the students so little power over their own writing. The answer must be inside the children, so I went to them.

I want the children to experience writing a How - To that is a little bit more abstract

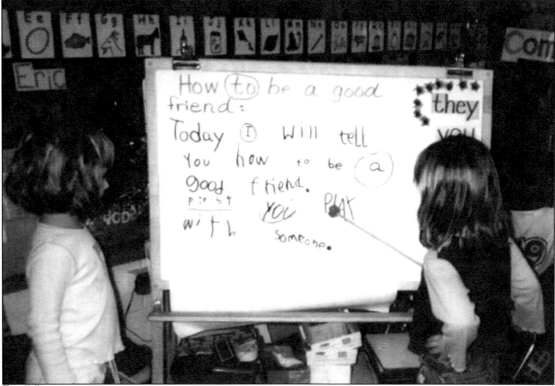

Fig. 7.5

than what they have done previously. I decide to hand the power of this decision over to the kindergarteners so that I can find out what *they* would like to write about. Being kindergarteners, many of the children are still very interested in writing about friends. The desire to play with friends, talk about friends, and write about friends is strong in the hearts of my five- year olds.

The children decide that we should give instructions on How to be a Good Friend. My hope is that each child has a very different piece, as each individual internalizes a varied idea of what is required to be a friend. I love that the children have their own ideas, and I want to support that. We read books about being a good friend, such as **A Cake all for ME!** by Karen Beil and *How To Lose All Your Friends* by Nancy Carlson, followed by Interactive Writing on the same topic. (Fig. 7.6 & 7.7)

Finally the students are free to write in their journals. The children take this task personally.

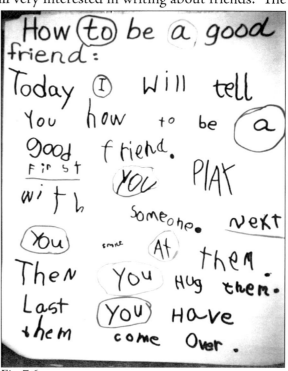

Fig. 7.6

Kim Dumaine

This first sample reads: (Fig. 7.7)

This is how you can be a friend.
You see a kid.
You go up to him.
Now you say hi.
Ask to be his friend. That is how I got to be friends with Cale.

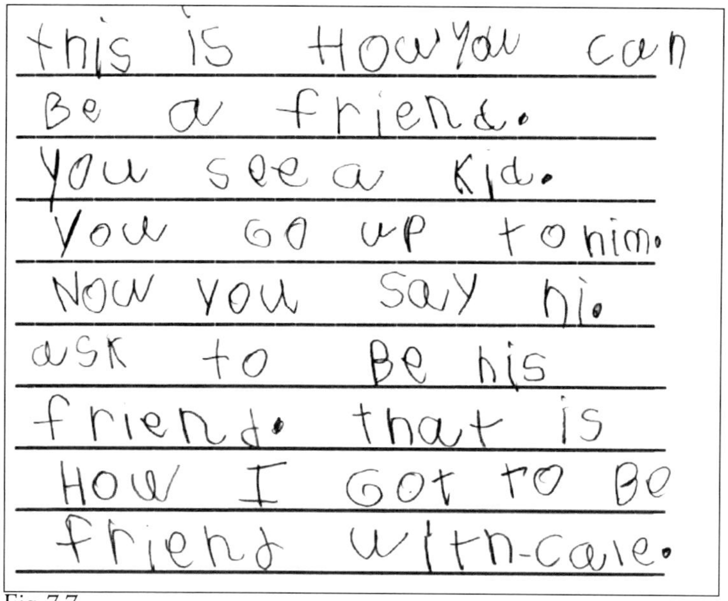

Fig. 7.7

Pierce gives us precise instructions on how to be a friend and validates his ideas in his closing sentence by explaining that he was able to gain a specific friend through his process.

Katherine chooses to utilize the sequencing words in her How-To:(Fig. 7.8)

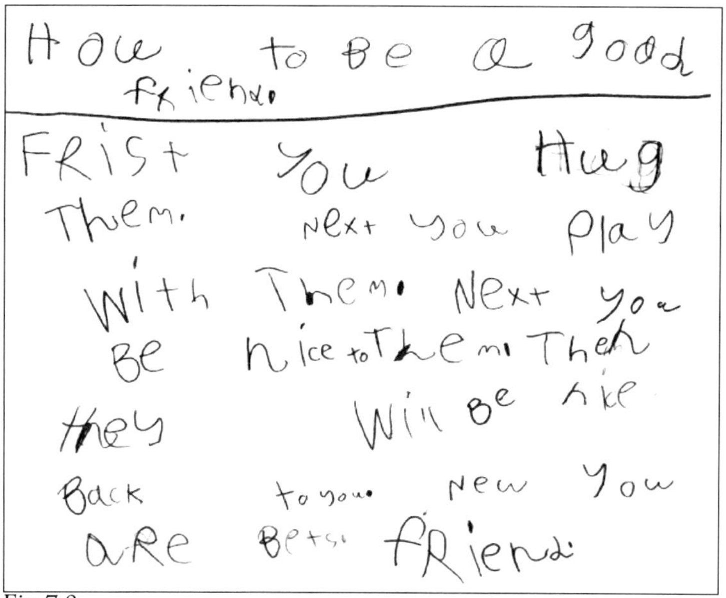

Fig. 7.8

How to be a good friend.

First you hug them. Next you play with them. Next you be nice to them. Then they will be nice back to you. Now you are best friends.

Eric relates his ideas through the use of a graphic organizer (Fig 7.9):

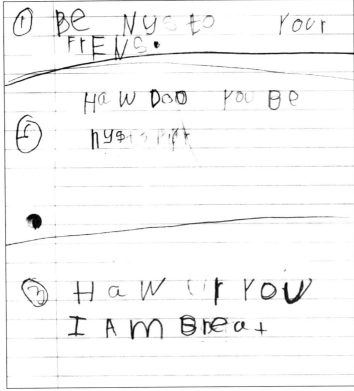

1 Be nice to your friends.
2 How do you be nice
3 How are you
   I am great

Fig. 7.8

    These pieces are versatile and individual. The kids are writing about something they care about, and it shows. Though it is early in the school year, the students feel that they are capable writers. This is evidenced in their expressive ideas. As the children share their ideas with one another, confidence grows along with enthusiasm. This is what I am hoping for. I have learned that I must always be on guard that I do not remove ownership from the author. I have also experienced that this can occur unintentionally, so I need to be sensitive to my teaching and modeling every moment. And I know that I can always go to my kids to straighten me out.

8 Descriptive Writing

The concept of descriptive writing is an idea that kindergarten students can easily grasp, if the teacher has been modeling it in her own writing. To make the learning concrete for my students, I have them make some sort of artistic creation to describe in writing. I find that the children take on more ownership when they write about something they have made themselves. Let's face it —we all do much better work when the topic is something we care about.

This is a lesson that is fun for the children and one that instills confidence. I think it works so well because children get excited by the preparation rather than by anything that I have done.

I bring in plenty of decorative supplies (glitter, stickers, paper, etc.) and let the students decorate construction paper snowmen (and women) in any manner that they choose. Making a unique snowman serves as an individualized prewriting experience. I give them plenty of time to complete their snow people. This can take up to thirty minutes, so it takes patience. I make use of this time by making my own snow person, which I will use later on when I model descriptive writing.

As the children finish up, I begin the lesson by telling the kids that I want to write about my snowman. I model that it needs to have an introduction. I say, "How can I start this off?" I take a few suggestions such as: "This is my snowman" and "My snow girl's name is….."

I choose one of the suggestions for myself. "This is my snowman." Now I begin my description. "He has a red hat. He also has three buttons, and black mittens. His orange nose is made from a carrot, and he has a raisin mouth." This is all modeled on chart paper. As I write, I explain to the kids that I am describing my snowman. I explain that for now I am describing what he looks like, but a description can also include information about what my snowman likes to do, what his personality is like, or any other information that describes my snowman. I decide to include," His name is Mr. White. He loves to drink ice water."

Now I solicit suggestions for a conclusion. I get plenty of, "Do you like him?" and, "I hope you like him." A few kids offer original suggestions, such as, "Let's go play snowball fight!" I choose one for myself and add it in. "Mr. White is super cool."

By now the students are excited about writing their descriptions. I give them paper to write on and they take off. Some of the students choose to prewrite in their journals (Fig. 8.1) prior to using the white paper that is offered.

Fig. 8.1

I walk around and conference with the students as they write. The youngsters love this project. All of my twenty-one kids are working. Upon completion, we all gather at the carpet. Several of the students are eager to share what they wrote. I hold up the snowperson as each child reads so that we can "check" to see if the snowman matched the writing. For publishing, we create a snow scene out in the hallway that includes every child's snow person and descriptive writing.

Cale's snowman (Fig. 8.2) is quite obviously a fan of the Texas Rangers baseball team. He has picked up that description is not solely about looks, but description can also include one's interests as well (Fig. 8.3). I can also see that Cale has chosen not to include an official conclusion. Conclusions can be tricky for kindergarteners, but I am now able to make note of this as a possible future conferencing point with Cale.

Fig. 8.2

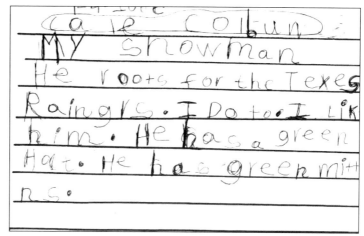

Fig. 8.3

Kate is still a minimal risk-taker in her writing, so descriptive writing has great appeal to her. Kate knows exactly what to do. She has a specific purpose for writing, follows it exactly, and completes it feeling successful (Fig. 8.5). These types of short, specific writing activities allow for children like Kate to practice her writing skills without the common, "I can't think of anything to write about" threat.

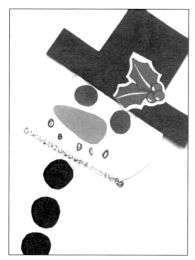

Fig. 8.4

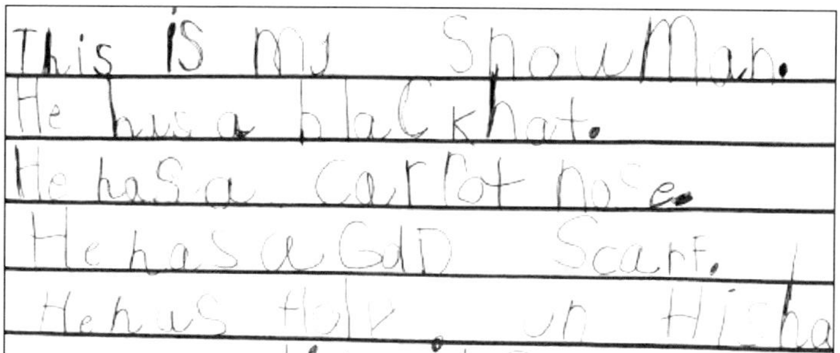

Fig. 8.5

I know that Kate will need special attention as the months proceed, in order to attain a greater level of comfort with herself as a writer. I will have to be delicate with Kate during conferences. My primary concerns will be building confidence in this child, and a greater cognition of her abilities.

The following are some good stories to build enthusiasm about student creations:
These books could be used to introduce the activity, or wrap up the process upon completion.

Snowballs	Louis Elhert
The Biggest Best Snowman Ever	Margery Cuyler
The Snowman Storybook (not *The Snowman*)	Raymond Briggs

9 Writing Narrative Birthday Stories

Five-Day Cycle – Usually taught beginning of January

Every young child can relate to having a birthday. Even if the child has never had a party, the chances are good that they have at least been to a birthday party. Kindergarten teachers are experts at celebrating the birthdays of their students, which ensures that five and six year olds are well equipped to write about birthdays. We write birthday narratives in January because several children have turned six by this point. I have also noticed that my students are more likely to stay with a piece and take it all the way to publishing if I am modeling this process within a time span that close to a week long; thus the five-day cycle.

DAY 1

I begin the five-day cycle with a read-aloud about a birthday. Some good birthday stories include:

Angelina's Birthday Surprise	Katherine Holibird
Arthur's Birthday	Marc Brown
A Birthday Cake for Little Bear	Max Velthuijs
Danny's Birthday	Edith Kunhardt
Happy Birthday, Jesse Bear!	Nancy White Carlstrom
Happy Birthday, Sam	Pat Hutchins
Happy Birthday to you!	Dr. Seuss
Mouse's Birthday	Jane Yolen
Mr. Elephant's Birthday Party	Jack Kent
The Secret Birthday Message	Eric Carle

(I usually place about twenty birthday books in the Book Browsing Center. Children will read these and get ideas for their own stories.)

After we read **Arthur's Birthday** on the first day of this cycle, I build interest by giving the students an artifact for their artifact bag, which is one birthday candle. (Each child in the classroom keeps an artifact, or souvenir, bag for the entire semester, in which small mementos from Writer's Workshop are stored.) Next I begin my own birthday story. I tell the children that I am going to make up a story about what "I hope" my husband, Mr. B, and my son, Stephen, will do when my birthday comes. In my class I have been encouraging the young writers to include dialogue in their stories, so I begin my lead with a quote. I model this as I write:

"Happy Birthday, Mom!" said Stephen

Then he gave me a box. No sound. (At this point I ask for help with the next sentence.

A child raises their hand and offers an idea, which we write interactively. I am pleased to notice the sentence includes dialogue.)

Stephen said, "Open it!"

(Now I go back to modeling.)

So I did. It was my favorite book. (Fig. 9.1)

Fig. 9.1

I tell the children that I will stop my story for now, but I will add more to it tomorrow. We follow this with a brainstorming session. Each child tells the class what they would like as a birthday present. I act as scribe as they shout out their gift ideas. (The class "wish list" will hang on the easel for the children to refer to when they create individual lists.) When the ideas are exhausted, I invite the students to create a personalized wish list. I have prepared a half sized sheet of paper for each child to list present ideas. This is the prewriting activity. My intention is to get the students revved up about creating personal narratives. Here are a few examples of the birthday lists my kindergarteners wrote during prewriting on day one:

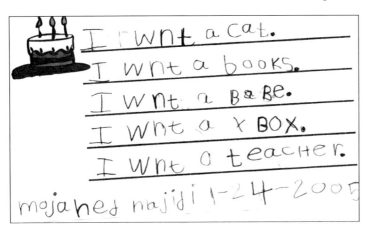

Fig. 9.2

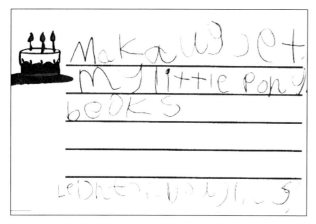

Fig. 9.3

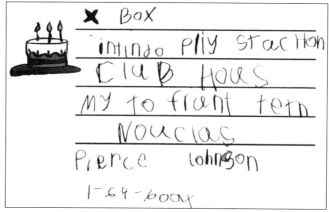

Fig. 9.4

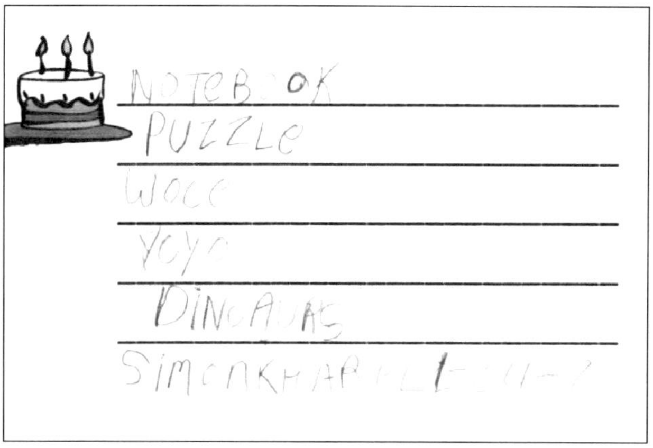

Fig. 9.5

DAY 2

I begin the second day with a different birthday story, *Happy Birthday Jesse Bear!* As a class we discuss some of the ideas that the author had, and think aloud about the possibility of anyone using any of these ideas. One child notices that Jesse Bear has games at his party, and thinks this is a good idea. I am certain to make note of the fact that Jesse Bear received a book as a gift, since the same thing occurred in my own narrative. I keep my promise from the previous day to go back to my own birthday story (Fig. 9.6). This time I invite the class to think up the first sentence of the day. We write the sentence interactively.

Fig. 9.6

I said "Thank you."

(I ask the class if I could please think of the next sentence myself.)

Then Stephen brought me breakfast. I write this sentence myself.

I stop after only two sentences and give the children their artifacts (balloons) because today will be the day that they begin their actual narratives and I want them to have plenty of writing time. I get the children excited by showing them fun "party paper" I have made for them to use to write their stories. As they write, I walk around the room with my conference clipboard and hold mini-conferences. Some of the children choose to write in their journals, rather than using the party paper. I realize that they want to get some ideas down before they commit to the cool paper, and this is their choice. Giving children the choice empowers them as writers.

DAY 3:

As always, I begin with another story involving a birthday. We choose *The Secret Birthday Message.* Again, we discuss good ideas that the author had. My class thinks Mr. Carle is smart to have the main character receive a puppy as a birthday gift. Before I ask the children to share their ideas for the upcoming sentence, we go back as a class and have a

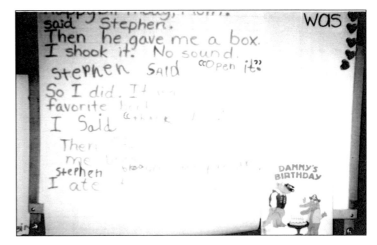

Fig. 9.7

shared reading of the story thus far, so as to be certain that our next sentence will flow along the story line. I invite the class to decide on the first sentence (Fig. 9.7) to add to our story today, which we write interactively.

> *Stephen brought me pancakes.*
> *(I take over the next sentence.)*
> *I ate them all.*

I stop here and give the students their artifacts (foil confetti) and their stories to continue working on. Today as I am walking around, I notice that some of the children are changing their minds about what they had previously written. A couple of the children are struggling with the possibility of making changes. I keep this in the back of my mind so that I can make a point of changing my own story on day four. I invite some of the children to share their writing with the entire class. Peers offer ideas for drafting or adding to these stories. "Maybe you could tell us what kind of present you got," Leighton offers. Simon considers her advice. We carefully put our work away until the next day.

DAY 4:

Of course, day four begins with another birthday story and discussion. As a class we re-read the model story. At this stage, I announce to the class that I want to make a change in my story. (Fig. 9.8) I tell the children that I really couldn't eat all of the pancakes my son made for me, so I take a black marker and draw a line through that sentence. I ask the class how many pancakes most of them could eat. The most popular number is two. I change my sentence:

I ate two of them.

Now I ask the class to think of a sentence, which we add interactively.

Mr. B. came in with some friends.

We read over the entire story thus far, and I give the children their papers to continue to work on. While conferencing, I notice that the children are more at ease about drafting and making changes. Most of the young writers bring their stories to a close on this day. These students will able to edit the following day. Again I ask some of the students to share their work, this time in small groups on the carpet.

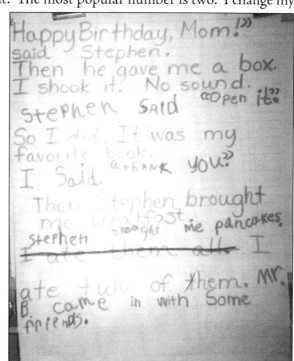
Fig. 9.8

DAY 5:

This will be the last day for me to model my birthday story. Most of the children will complete their own birthday stories, but a few continue into the following week. As always, I begin with a birthday read-aloud and discussion. We then reread the model story. I begin by choosing this sentence myself:

> Nobody brought me a present.

After I write this sentence, I begin a discussion as to why nobody who came to the party brought me a present. We talk about being with the people you love being the most important thing. We talk about the fact that my son had already given me a gift, and I actually reveal this gift for the kids to see. I talk about the hard work my husband put into that day, inviting friends to come over, and making party preparations. Finally I admit that my story is not entirely fictional. Mr. B. really did have a surprise party for me. I explained how happy it made me feel to see all the people that love me. I am preparing the kids to come up with an appropriate closing sentence. I admit that I am leading my children toward a conclusion that follows along the story line. I want the class to have a feel for what is going on inside my head as I think (aloud). I ask the children to help me out with my ending. Yitzi says, "It was a fun day." Akram offers, "I liked my party." Both of these are fine conclusions, but I keep taking suggestions, hoping for a closing that is personal to my narrative (Fig. 9.9). Katherine gives us an idea:

> My present was a party.

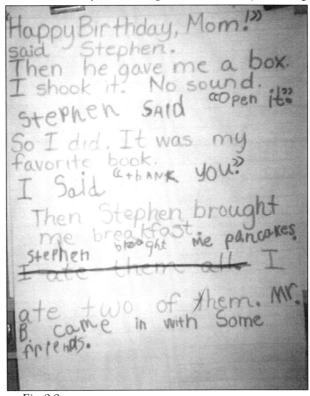

Fig. 9.9

As a class, we agree on this ending, which we write interactively.

The children go back into their work at their various stages. Many are drafting/editing. Many of the students complete their stories. For publishing, the students read their stories to the entire class and use the Pointing strategy (in which listeners point out parts they like, as described on page 151 of *Acts of Teaching*, by Carroll and Wilson. Later, students also read to office personnel. Finally, these stories will be given colorful folders and posted in the hallway. Several of the children have developed strong endurance and have completed lengthy stories.

Fig. 9.10

Fig. 9.11

Fig. 9.12

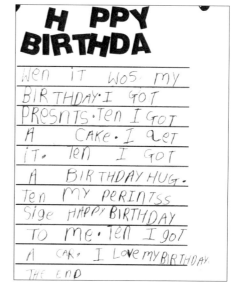

Fig. 9.13

This five-day cycle exemplifies the capabilities of our youngest learners! Even five-year olds can continue to work on the same piece for several days, especially if they have been taught writing is a process that can continue over a span of many days. January is a wonderful time during the kindergarten year. This is when the children are bursting with ideas, and their confidence has been built to the point they are adept, independent writers. Mid-year is a joyful time to be a kindergarten teacher of writing. My role switches from teacher to facilitator. Rather than helping kids sound out words, we conference about ideas. The students no longer need me in the same capacity. They are able to strike out on their own and begin writing about topics they care about. Rarely do I ever hear, "I can't think of anything to write about." Mid-year I begin to enjoy the fruit of the seeds planted all semester long. The children utilize the skills they have acquired all semester. They know how to apply these skills. And best of all, they enjoy applying these skills.

10 Writing Narratives

Writing with Story Components

My kindergarteners are fairly independent writers by late December and early January. This is a good time to learn the narrative. Throughout the semester, I have been carefully choosing read alouds that contain the following four components:

1. main character (or characters)
2. easily identifiable setting (time & place)
3. problem
4. solution

After I have read several stories that model these components throughout the previous few weeks, I ask the children to find and identify these components daily, following each read aloud. I point out to the children that this is how good authors write stories. I make this point over and over again after each read aloud. Using authors as models through the school year helps the children to have a personal connection with the stories that they read. In turn, the youngsters are comfortable using components that they see in the stories that they read. Young children can easily see the need to include a main character in their own stories, since they have made a connection with stories that include main characters in their everyday reading. Once young writers notice the setting in several of their favorite books, they incorporate settings into their own original works.

Over a ten-day span of time, we use Interactive Writing to create a class-made narrative about a snowman.

Fig. 10.1

Fig. 10.2

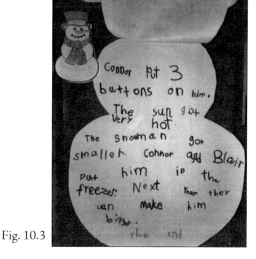

Fig. 10.3

This way, I have used authors to model elements I want the kids to use, and now, I have used peer modeling. During this ten-day span of time, children are putting their thoughts down in their journals as prewriting.

Once each child has had ample prewriting time, he or she begins to craft narratives independently. I give the students blank snowman-shaped books to write in, so that they can feel like real authors. I ask them to wait and add the title to their front covers when the story is complete. This is a part of the publishing process.

As the children are writing their stories, I am able to walk around the room and conference with individuals. Occasionally a child will want to refer to one of the snowman narratives that we used as a read aloud. These books are always out in a specific spot in the room. I try to pay attention to the books that are chosen by the students, so that I can discern which books make good mentor texts (published children's books from which students can glean ideas to use when crafting their own writing). It is sometimes a good idea to purchase additional copies of class favorites.

Good "snow" books that illustrate kindergarten level story components:

Snow Family	Daniel Kirk
Snowmen at Night	Caralyn Buehner
Snow	Uri Shulevitz
The Biggest Best Snowman	Margery Cuyler

As I conference, I also make note of students with interesting ideas that I will later ask them to share with the class. At the conclusion of each day's writer's workshop, we conduct a sharing time. Some kids will wish to read their pieces even if they are unfinished so that they can solicit ideas from peers. Student authors request questions and comments from the class about each piece. Listeners share what they like about the piece and what they want to know more about. This technique, called Say Back, is fully explained on page 157 of *Acts of Teaching*, by Carroll and Wilson. This helps the young authors to see their stories from the point of view of their audience.

When each child has completed his/her draft and is ready to publish, each decorates the front cover of the snowman book and gives it a title. After reading their entire story to the class, the kids can then read their stories to the office personnel, and I post them outside the room (if the child chooses). My biggest problem occurs when the office calls my room and asks me to stop sending down so many authors!

Shelby's Story (Fig. 10. & 10.5):

The Snowgirl

One day it was snowing. Me an my sister went downstairs. I opened the door. It was snowing! We made a snowgirl. We pushed and packed and rolled and stacked. Now we have a snowgirl. I put a nose on her. I put

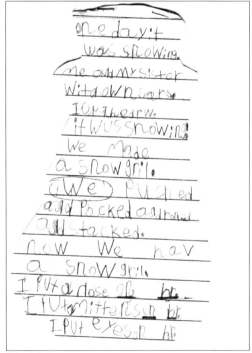

Fig. 10.4

mittens on her. I put eyes on her. I put a mouth on her. it melted. but. it was OK. I was so happy because I made another snowgirl. It was a great day. I put ice on her. She is OK. The end

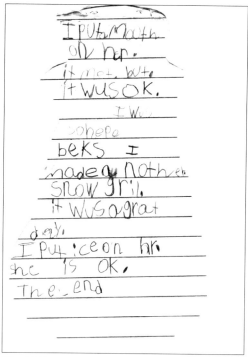

Fig. 10.5

Notice the sentence, "We pushed and packed and rolled and stacked." This sentence is a variation very close to a sentence from one of the read-alouds that was used as a mentor text. Shelby liked the rhythm of this sentence and found a way to make a place for it in her story.

Kate's Story:

The Snowman Story

One day I looked outside the window. I saw snow. I went out. Me and Leighton built a snowman. Then We put on

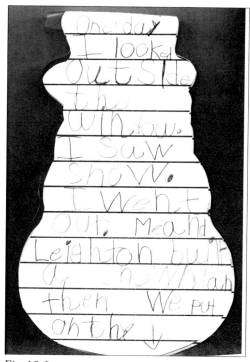

Fig. 10.6

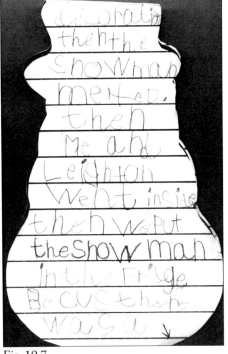

Fig. 10.7

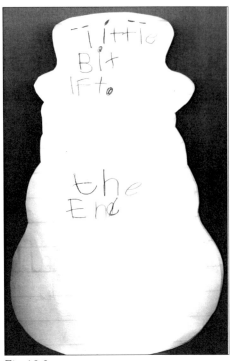

Fig. 10.8

the decorations. Then the snowman melted. Then me and Leighton went inside. Then we put the snowman in the fridge because there was a little bit lft.

THE END

While conferencing with Kate, I am able to talk with her about the frequent use of the word "then" in her story. We are able to count together and discover that this word is used four times. We talk about optional words that could be used instead of "then." But because I know that Kate is sensitive about correction, I do not ask her to make any changes. This is Kate's story, not mine. I want Kate to be happy with her accomplishment. Right now, self-confidence is the first priority.

Cale's Story (Fig. 10.10-10.12):

the Best snow Man

Fig. 10.9

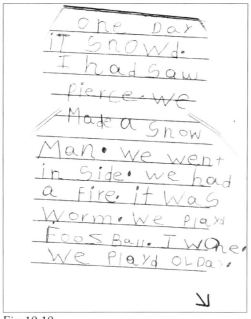
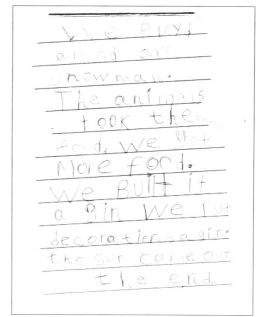

Fig. 10.10   Fig. 10.8

One Day iT snowd. I had saw Pierce. We Made a snow Man.
We went inside. We had a Fire. It was worm. We playd Foozball.
I wone. We Playd oL Day. We played around are snowman. **
The animals took the food. We got more food. We built it a gin.
We put decorations a gin. the sun came out. The end

*For clarification: The "problem" in Cale's story is that he and his friend, Pierce, decorated their "Best Snowman" with food. Animals then came along and took the food, which Cale and Pierce replaced after rebuilding the destroyed snowman. Had I not conferenced with Cale, I would not be privy to this information. This helps me as a teacher. I now know that I need to nudge this child (on his next piece) to include all-important details. I can note this on my conference clipboard so that I will be reminded during our next conference.

This is one of the first times in the school year that I push most of my kids to go through the entire process of writing. After daily modeling, the children begin by using their journals for prewriting. After establishing a level of comfort with their stories, they move onto the snowman shaped books. While writing in these book, they are able to experience drafting, editing, and conferencing. Finally, students may experience publishing through the creation of a title, decorating their front cover, and reading their story to an audience. Prior to this point in the school year, I allow my kids to direct how far they will take each piece. However, I find that there is always a delicate balance involved in allowing each child the freedom to pursue learning at an individual rate. I need to be certain that I know each student well. I need to know when the time comes to gives each child the nudge they may need to "take it to the next level." This is why conferencing is such an extremely valuable tool for me as a kindergarten teacher.

11 Writing Letters

Students in kindergarten enjoy

writing letters. Some kindergarten students feel more comfortable writing letters than any other type of writing. Letters have a special meaning, since they always have a specific audience. Each child knows that he or she is writing a letter to a specific and special person, which makes the act of writing that letter meaningful. We usually write our very first letter as an entire class, and this takes place early in the school year (Fig. 11.1).

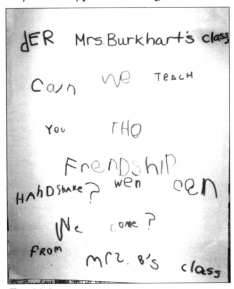

Fig. 11.1

I introduce the concept of letter writing to the entire class using Interactive Writing. To begin, I set the purpose: I have recently taught my class a "friendship handshake." (This idea is an offshoot from *Interactive Writing* by McCarrier, Pinnell, and Fountas, in which one class writes to ask another class if they would like to learn the Butterfly Handshake.) I ask the children in my class if they think it would be fun to teach this handshake to another kindergarten class, and of course, they do. So I tell my kindergarteners that we could write the other class a letter, asking them if they would like to learn this handshake. Since I am mainly interested in teaching the concept of letter writing at this introductory stage, we do not talk about the components of a proper letter, such as heading, greeting, body, closing, and signature; those will come later. The above letter was written in September, so I am concerned with mainly content (and of course, the letter/sound relationship). As a class we discuss what our letter should say. I guide the children to choose short, simple sentences, as I know we are still learning to "say the sounds" as we write. As a class we decide what to say, and we write it interactively. At this point in the school year, there is no drafting, editing, or correcting of any kind. We practice reading our letter using shared reading. As a precursor to publishing (which will come later in the school year) we take our letter over to our friends' class and read it to them, again as a shared reading. There is a reward involved. The next day we receive a return letter from our friends, telling us the time to come into their class. We are then able to teach our new friends the "friendship handshake."

I also like to use field trips as a chance to write a thank you letter as a class. In the example here, our class went on a field trip to our district's Environmental Center (Fig. 12.2). We were able to observe all sorts of living things, such as animals and plant life, including a class favorite—the Ear Fungus plant. Upon our return, we created a thank you note, using Interactive Writing, and each child illustrated his or her favorite attraction. This takes place very early in the school year, so I am still introducing the concept of a letter to the kids. We are still not concerned with all the letter components. We are more concerned with sending a message of thanks.

Later on in the school year, I return to letter writing in greater depth. This usually takes place in early December. Again, the purpose is to speak to a specific audience, which is exactly why I choose this time during the school year. We practice by writing all types of letters, including letters to Mom and Dad (Fig. 11.3 & 11.4).

Fig. 11.2

Fig. 11.1

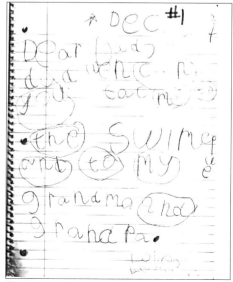

Fig. 11.4

But our ultimate audience will be Santa Claus. This time around I do teach the students the five components of a proper letter and each components' name. I also teach them a hand signal to accompany each name. For the heading, we pat our heads. For the greeting, we wave back and forth. For the body, we rub our bellies (I could only get away with this in kindergarten). For the closing, we close our hands together like a book. For the signature, we hold "air pencils" up and scribble out our names into the air. These Kinesthetic movements aid in the memory of the components that I want the students to remember. After we practice by writing letters to our friends and family members, we write a Santa letter using Interactive Writing.

Fig. 11.5

Fig. 11.6

Above are samples of Interactively written class letters to Santa, done by the past two years' kindergarten classes. These show the different ideas and personalities of each class.

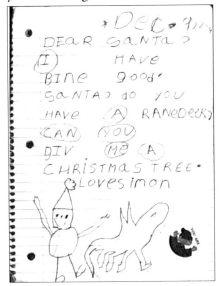

Fig. 11.7

Some teachers do not feel that much writing as a process can really take place during letter writing. For example, what can be done for prewriting? Actually, prewriting can take place, even when writing letters. And children can choose how they would like to do that prewriting. One option is that children first write a "practice" letter (Fig. 11.7) in their journals, before using the actual "Santa Stationery" that will later be mailed off.

Another prewriting option is to for the children to make a "wish list" of items that they would like to ask for. This list can then be used as a reference when the students are drafting the letter to Santa (Figs. 11. 8).

This prewriting list asks for:

1. X Box 360
2. Sorry (the board game)
3. a dog

Fig. 11.8

The letter (Fig. 11.9) makes reference to some, but not all, of the items listed. This shows the thought process of the child. He decides to add a little more conversation and voice to his letter, rather than sounding greedy by only asking for things for himself without having anything nice to say to Santa (something we discuss in class).

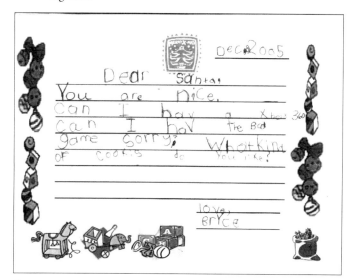

Fig. 11.9

This prewriting list asks for:

> G I Joe
> gameboy
> Frisbee
> **Harry Potter and the Goblet of Fire**

This child also opts to leave a few of the "list" items out of his letter (Fig. 11.11) in favor of conversation, yet he adds an item not on the previous list: a hamster! So thinking about writing can take place during letter writing, just as drafting and editing can take place during letter writing. As the children work to compose their letters, I walk around my students and drop in on those that need conferences, and

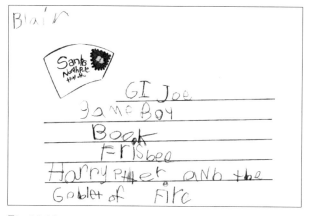

Fig. 11.10

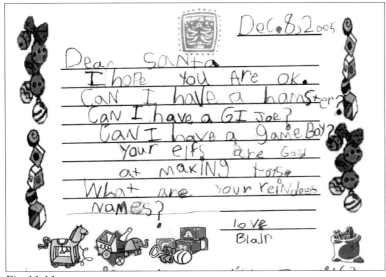

Fig. 11.11

help them out as far as ideas for drafting, or help them notice when (or if) editing is required. This is a time that knowing my students well is necessary. There are some items that I will not ask certain children to edit, depending on where they are with mechanics skills. Also, sometimes a teacher just knows when a child needs a break. It is often unwise to "edit a paper to death." In so doing, I could also "edit the writer to death."

A fun part is the publishing. Once the children have completed their letters on their special paper, we mail them off to Santa, who always writes back. The wonderful fourth grade teacher at my school, Ms. Linda Hubbard, gives the letters that my kids have written to her own students. She asks her fourth grade writers to create a "Genuine Letter from Santa" for each one of my students, often even matching her fourth graders up with letters from specific kindergarteners that they may know, or be related to. This way each child in my class is able to receive a very personalized letter back from Santa.

Kindergarten students also enjoy writing letters to soldiers overseas. I use the Internet to show my students photographs of soldiers living and working overseas, in order to give them a sense of familiarity and kinship with these soldiers. Ultimately, I would love to see my students expressing interest in the soldiers' lives, and perhaps even expressing gratitude. This is the reason that I want my children to see photos and videos of soldiers. It is important for the children to have some knowledge about their audience, and this serves as yet another form of prewriting at the kindergarten level. Of course, we also create a class-made letter interactively (Fig. 11.12).

Fig. 11.12

The purpose here is to get the children into a discussion about what they might want to say to their soldier, or what kinds of questions they wish to ask. As with the Santa letters, I remind the youngsters that it is important to let the person we are writing know that we care about them and that they are special. We can do this by asking them about their lives and by telling them that we care about them. This helps the children to individualize each letter. I tell them that the soldiers would be bored if 22 letters came from a kindergarten classroom, and each one said exactly the same thing. The children draft their letters in the usual manner, with conferences as needed.

We then share our letters aloud with our classmates, in order to ensure that our letters are not too similar (Figs. 11.13 & 11.14).

In this way, young children can conference with each other. Some teachers feel that kindergarteners are too young to conference with one another. I believe it can be done as long as children are sharing ideas, rather than correcting each other's writing. I agree that young children should not edit each other's work, but I notice children will often "piggyback" off one another's thoughts, which can spur better ideas and adds to our cohesiveness as a class of writers.

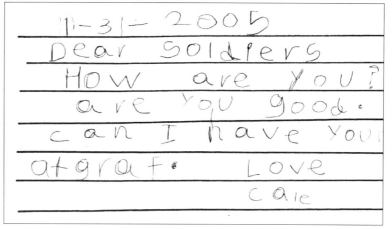

Fig. 11.11

Fig. 11.11

Writing letters is a fun activity that can take place at any time throughout the entire school year. I love to read the students' letters along the way as they mature as writers and as people. Starting off simple, with an obvious purpose and audience, is the best way to introduce letter writing to an entire class. Once the children see the value of letter writing, it is easy to teach the finer points of writing letters —such as including conversation, or even the importance of including the heading, greeting, body, closing, and signature. And sometimes, in the years when I'm lucky, my kindergarten students will remember me and send me letters from their first grade classrooms.

Here is an example of a first grader who has written a letter (Fig. 11.15) to a kindergarten friend during the first week of school.

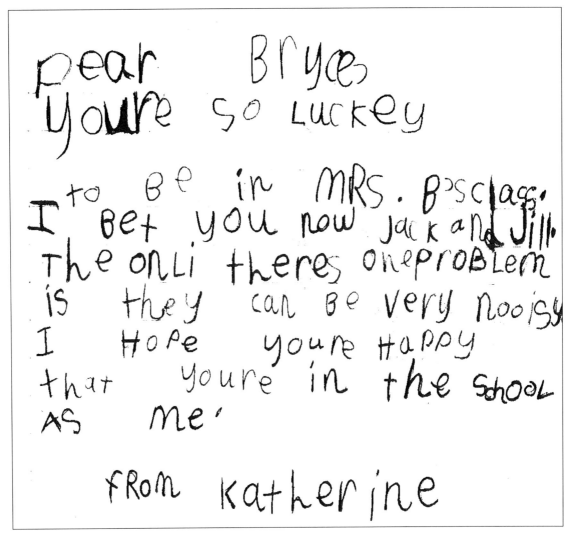

Fig. 11.15

Katherine has written to her young friend Bryce upon his entry into my kindergarten class. She lets him know how lucky he is, and then warns him about our noisy class birds, Jack and Jill. Katherine has initiated this task on her own. It is not a class assignment. Katherine has adopted a valuable skill that she will be able to use all her life.

12 Writing in Subject Areas

Writing in Science

Many kindergarten teachers must contend with extreme time limits on their teaching, such as half-day programs. This causes the various subject areas to compete for the precious time allotted in a shortened schedule. For years, kindergarten teachers have integrated instruction to solve this problem. Writing in the various subject areas is a way to cover writing skills, reading skills, and even a third subject area, such as math, science, health, or social studies.

As kindergarten teachers, we are required to include the study of water in our science curriculum. Students' writing can be used as a tool to ascertain their knowledge on the subject, and makes documentation easier. Teachers can look over student writing to decide if the children have mastered the desired information, or if lessons require re-teaching.

In my own kindergarten classroom, we write throughout the entire water unit. The children use science journals to record learning. The student samples below cover "Uses for Rain." Some books that I like to use in my own water unit include:

Water Dance	Thomas Locke
I Am Water	Jean Marzollo
Rain	Rozanne Williams
Down Comes the Rain	Franklin M. Branley

The books facilitate discussions on the knowledge gained by the children. These discussions can become a prewriting experience for the kids.

For example, the students break up into small groups to discuss "uses of rain" before coming together as a class to share findings. Many of the students will come up to the white board to brainstorm in front of the class. Other kids will "piggyback" off of a friend's idea, which will lead to further discussion, and thus to the listing of more ideas.

Next, the children individually write about the uses of rain (Fig. 12.1). The students read their pieces to one another and add more information to their pieces. While this is going on, I walk around and conference with individuals. We discuss drafting and editing, depending upon the needs of each child.

Fig. 12.1

Fig. 12.2

Finally, we will reconvene as an entire class. Individual students share their pieces as desired. I then invite the students to mount their pieces on a giant construction paper raindrop. For publishing, all of the raindrops will be combined into a class made book, which is placed in the reading center. (Each year my goal is to have between twenty and twenty-five class made books in the reading center. These make a wonderful gift for each child to take home on the last day of school.)

As a class, we also create a "Rain" poem (Fig. 12.2) using Interactive Writing, which we present to the school principal. Ending certain units with a fun poem creates a great memory for the kids, both about the subject taught and about the experience of writing itself.

Graphic organizers, such as T-charts (Figs. 12.3 & 12.4) are helpful in getting young children thinking about science concepts. The process of completing a T-chart can take several days, or only a few days if my class is under a time constraint.

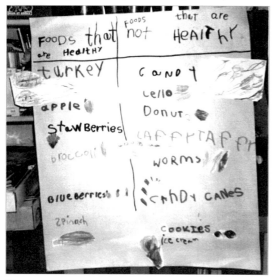

Fig. 12.3

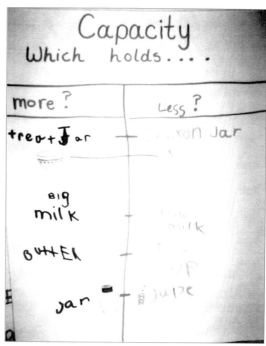

Fig. 12.4

As individual students come up to add their information to the T-chart, the students that are looking on have white boards and markers, in order to "write along" with the child up at the chart. This way every child is included in the experience. The charts are later laminated and hung in the science center.

In my classroom we spend several weeks learning the concept of living vs. nonliving. A class T-chart is created to display knowledge of living things and nonliving things (Figs. 12.5 & 12.6).

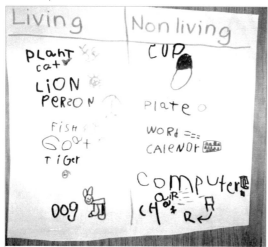

Fig. 12.5

Fig. 12.6

Fig. 12.7

We also list the Needs of Living Things (Fig. 12.7).

As a class, we decide that plants and trees are living things, and include them in our unit. We grow our own baby "trees." Over the course of the school year, we create a scrapbook about trees. Most of the pages in this book consist of Interactive Writing samples, such as the ones seen here (Figs. 12.8 & 12.9), and individual student writing.

Fig. 12.8

Fig. 12.9

As a class we chart out the parts of a tree (Fig. 12.10), again using Interactive Writing. I use this chart in the science center by placing Velcro™ dots on the chart with the "names of the parts of a tree" typed on them, so that the children can label the parts of a tree on the tree chart.

The children can enjoy labeling the parts of a tree over and over again as long as this cart remains in the science center (Fig.12.11). This is a perfect example of one way that writing can be taking place in all the kindergarten centers throughout the year.

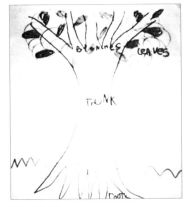

Fig. 12.10

Fig. 12.11

Fig. 12.12

Texas kindergarten curriculum also mandates learning life cycles of different living things. Writing is an instrument that helps children share their acquired knowledge of various life cycles. (Asking students to write about what they know also helps with parent conferences, as I always have evidence of student learning on hand to refer to.) I can look at the piece below to examine if my student grasps the concept of "How a frog egg becomes a frog" after we have studied their life cycles by reading about them, writing about them interactively (fig. 12.13), and growing our own frog in class(fig. 12.14).

Fig. 12.13

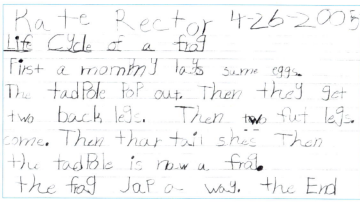

Fig. 12.14

Kindergarten students love to work with life cycles because this knowledge can be applied to class pets and growing plants. Growing butterflies from caterpillars is fun for the students and easy for me. Kits for growing butterflies can be bought from many science catalogs, or even through the Internet. While we wait for our butterflies to emerge, we read books on butterfly life cycles, watch videos showing butterflies emerge, and research butterflies on the Internet. After the experience of watching our butterflies go through the entire life cycle, we set them free. We begin to write about the experience of the caterpillar going through all of its changes (Figs. 12.15-12.17)

Fig. 12.15

Fig. 12.16

Fig. 12.17

In the photos (Figs. 12. 15-12.17), the students have cutout shapes (cut by me to save time) that resemble butterflies for the covers of their butterfly books. Once all of the students have gone through the publishing process, we create a scene outside the room on the wall of our butterfly books "flying through a garden".

The students also write a personal narrative explaining their own growth process, or lifecycle (fig. 12.18). This way I know that they can take the knowledge they have gained and apply it to themselves. I also get a kick out of reading the students' own versions of their growth processes. A great book to stir up thinking is *How Have I Grown*, by Mary Reid.

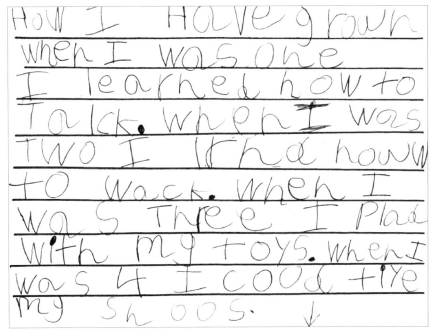

Fig. 12.18

These science/ writing activities show just a tiny snapshot of what can be done to combine science and writing in a kindergarten classroom. As teachers, we are limited only by own imagination. For every science experiment, concept, or activity, there is writing that can take place. Writing helps embed learned material into the memories of our students. Writing allows students to use their creativity. And writing offers instant documentation to teachers.

Writing in Social Studies

Writing is a great way for children to show what they know in terms of recalling facts. Writing also helps these facts stick in the memory. I have found that children will retain information that they have recorded in writing far longer than they can recall information they are simply asked to "know."

In February and March, I conduct a study unit covering The United States of America, including symbols, presidents, and important people that shaped our nation. This may seem like a dry subject for five year olds, but I believe their excitement for learning these topics is evidenced in their writing. As kindergarten teachers in the state of Texas, this is part of our state mandated curriculum, so I figure I am going to have fun with my students while learning about America.

I usually begin by taking my class to the website whitehouse.gov. We go to the "kids" section. From there children can learn many exciting and personal facts about the current president. These are points of interest for children. I show the students all of the different rooms in the White House, such as the blue room, the red room, the oval office, the indoor pool, movie theater, etc. The students love getting this inside view.

I read the nonfiction book *The White House* by Susan H. Gray to the class. As a whole group, we brainstorm facts about the White House from the website and the book. Then I ask each child to draw a large picture of the White House. In the windows of the White House, I ask the kids to write facts about the White House. The kids really enjoy this fun activity, which actually serves as a graphic organizer (Fig. 15.1).

Fig. 12.19

The facts included in this particular piece are:
It has a red room. It has a green room. It has a red room.
Once the White House had a fire. But it rained.
The White House has 132 rooms.
Every Easter visitors come.
They have a dog named Barney.
It has a bowling room.
The White House is very special.

This type of writing allows for each child's individuality. Every child chooses the facts that they find most important or most interesting. It also serves as a quick assessment for me.

Next we read books about the current President. There are some wonderful nonfiction books that appeal to kindergarteners, which are published by Compass Point Books. The name of the series is *Let's See*. (In fact, the entire series includes stories about everything in America, from the flag to voting to important places – all at a kindergarten level.) We will read these types of books for several days while the students record thoughts in their journals about the president and the presidency. This serves as their prewriting. Soon I will begin to ask them to think a little deeper and put themselves in the imaginary position of being the President. There are a number of stories that aid in jump-starting these discussions:

Duck for President	Doreen Cronin
Max for President	Jarrett J. Krooczka
My Teacher for President	Kay Winters

After much discussion and prewriting, I will pose the question, "What do you think the president does all day?" I offer the children special presidential paper, which I create on my computer. Here are a few of the students' responses (Fig 12.20-12.22):

Fig. 12.20

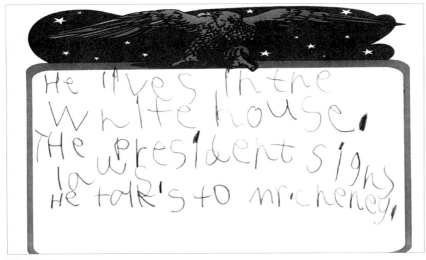

Fig. 12.21

The following day we discuss the idea of being the President. I ask the children to imagine that they are each running for the position of President, just as Max did in the story *Max for President*. I invite each child to create

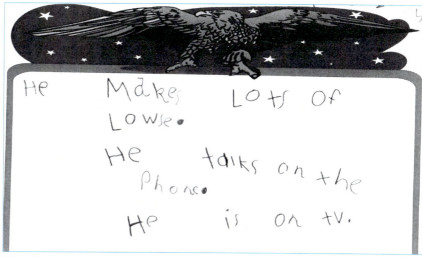

Fig. 12.22

a badge (Fig. 12.23) that completes the sentence, "If I were president…."

Fig. 12.23

This badge reads:

    If I were President…….
    I would help my school. I would make houses clean. I would sign important papers. I would watch Disney channel every night. I would make rides safe.

We hang these badges (which can be created on any computer) around the room after the students share their ideas. These badges can lead to great discussions as to whom we might choose to vote for, based on their plans as President.

At this time in my particular district, kindergarten writing skills are assessed before going on to first grade. This test is always a retelling (Each student is asked to read a particular story, and retell the events of the story on paper, in sequential order). I work a retelling into every study unit that I possibly can, so that the assessment will not be unexpected to the children. By the end of the kindergarten year, the children will have written so many retellings that this assessment is usually no problem. One story that serves as a great platform for a retelling is ***Arthur Meets the President***, by Marc Brown. After reading this story aloud, we do a mock retelling, verbally. This gets the mental muscles pumping. I will call on someone to tell, "What happened in the beginning? What happened in the middle? What happened at the end?" This gets the kids in gear and ready to write.

Since this is an early version of an evaluation, I want to see the kids' raw work. I try to assist the students as little as possible, so that I can later use these pieces to evaluate the strengths and needs of each child. These retellings give me plenty of information about each child.

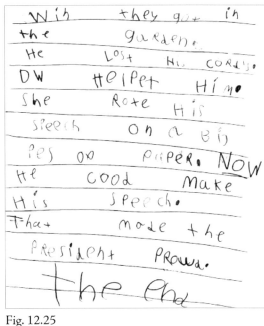

Fig. 12.24   Fig. 12.25

The first retelling (Figs 12.24 & 12.25) reads:

> Arthur's teacher was saying there is going to be a writing contest. The winner will get to go to the White House. Arthur won. The Whole class got on a airplane. Athur was scared. When they went to the White house. Athur began to sweat. When they got in the garden he lost his cards. D.W. helped him. She wrote his ' speech on a big piece of paper. <u>NOW</u> he could make his speech. That made the president proud. The end.

The information I get from this retelling lets me know that this student has an excellent understanding of what the story entails. She may not know all the rules of grammar and spelling, but she is not expected to know them. This child is an exceptional writer. She shows good use of voice. Her sequencing is compatible with the story line. She does not get bogged down with unimportant details.

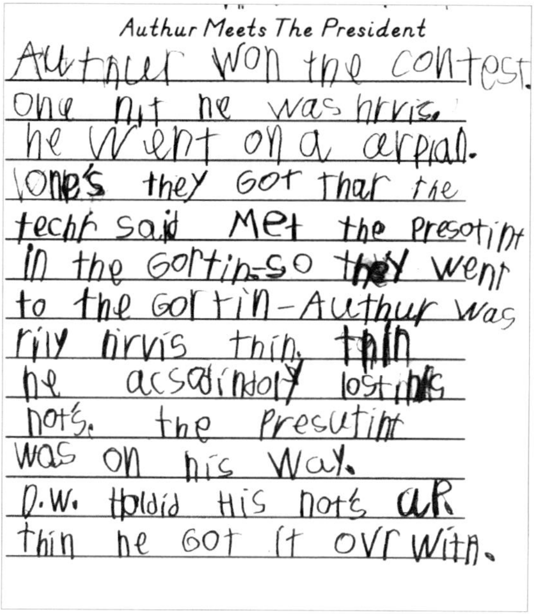

Fig. 12.25

The second retelling (Fig. 12.15) reads:

> Author won the contest. One night he was nervous. He went on a airplane. Once they got there the teacher said meet the president in the garden — so they went to the garden — Arthur was really nervous then. Then he accidentally lost his notes. The president was on his way. D.W. holded his notes up. Then he got it over with.

This student is also quite an excellent writer. I need to help him a little bit with his sequencing so that he does not give away the ending straight away. Also, he needs to work on the natural flow of his retelling. However, I can tell that this student understands the concept of recalling the story well, and is a fine writer.

The children also learn and write about other important American Presidents, such as Abraham Lincoln and George Washington. As we read about each President, we will interactively add facts about the two important men to our class Venn diagram (Fig 12.27), noting similarities and differences between the two Presidents. There are many wonderful books for kids about both Lincoln and Washington, but the absolute must haves are ***A Picture Book of Abraham Lincoln*** and ***A Picture Book of George Washington***, both by David A. Adler.

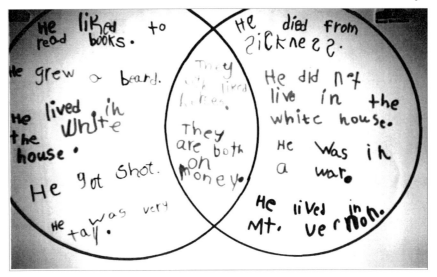

Fig. 12.27

I devote a full week to each President. Each day includes nonfiction stories about the specific President. The children write in their journals about the particular President, either Lincoln or Washington, and I walk around with my clipboard and have conferences. I also give the students artifacts for their artifact bags, which consist of fake pennies and fake quarters. Each day one or two kids will share their journal entries with the rest of the class. The person doing the sharing will accept questions and comments from their peers. This helps develop the writing skills of the entire class as they add information, draft, and edit. Finally, to publish, each child chooses one favorite President (Figs. 12.28 & 12.29) to write about and turn into a final product by using special American Stationery, as pictured here. (I purchase this special paper at my local office supply store.)

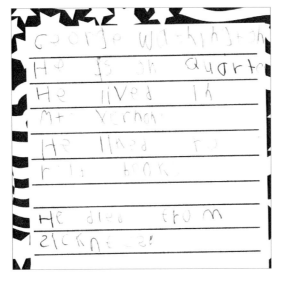

Fig. 12.28

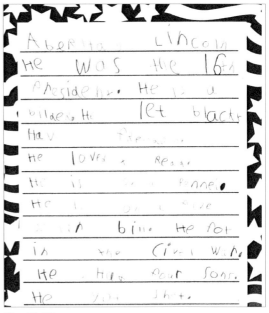

Fig. 12.29

Kim Dumaine

Important American symbols are a part of this unit as well. One such symbol that kindergarteners find interesting is the Liberty Bell. A wonderful book full of interesting facts is ***The Liberty Bell***, by Gail Sakurai. After reading about the Liberty Bell, small group discussions work well because students can discuss interesting facts in more depth. I am always fascinated with some of the tiny details that certain children will find to be extremely important. When we return as a whole group, the children brainstorm important facts about the Liberty Bell, (Fig 12.30) which we write interactively. Next the children write their own accounts of the important facts about the Liberty Bell. Once the piece is completed, they may create their own artistic version of the Liberty Bell, complete with the crack. The child attaches the art(Fig. 12.31) to the writing for a published work.

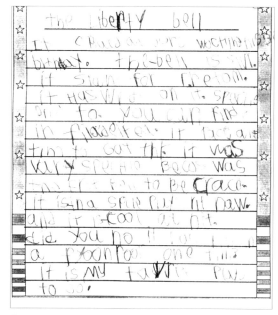

Fig. 12.30

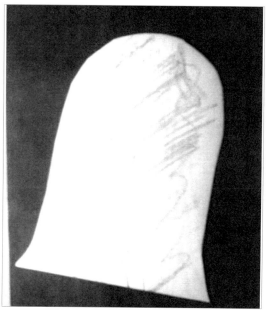

Fig. 12.31

This particular piece reads:
The Liberty Bell
*It cracked on George Washington's birthday.
The bell is silver. It stands for freedom.
It has words on it. Special one's too. You
can find it in Philadelphia. It takes a long time
to get there. It was very special because it was
the first bell to be cracked. It is in a special
place right now. And it is cool at night. Did
you know it has been in a funeral one time?
It is my favorite place to go.*

Of course the most exciting American symbol is the Statue of Liberty. The children get so excited when they find out that people can actually go up inside her. Three great books on this topic are *The Statue of Liberty* by Lucille Recht Penner, *The Statue of Liberty* by Patricia Ryon Quiri, and *The Statue of Liberty* by Dana Meachen Rau.

I repeat the same learning process with the Statue of Liberty as I did with the Liberty Bell. We allow time for discussion before writing begins. I also ask the students to talk about the reasons why the Statue is important. Akram tells us the Liberty Bell "stands for freedom." Rachel informs the class that "lots of kids go there on field trips." The children go into their journals for prewriting and drafting following our discussion. Then the students write about the Statue, and turn that writing into a published work (Fig. 12.32) using special paper from the writing center.

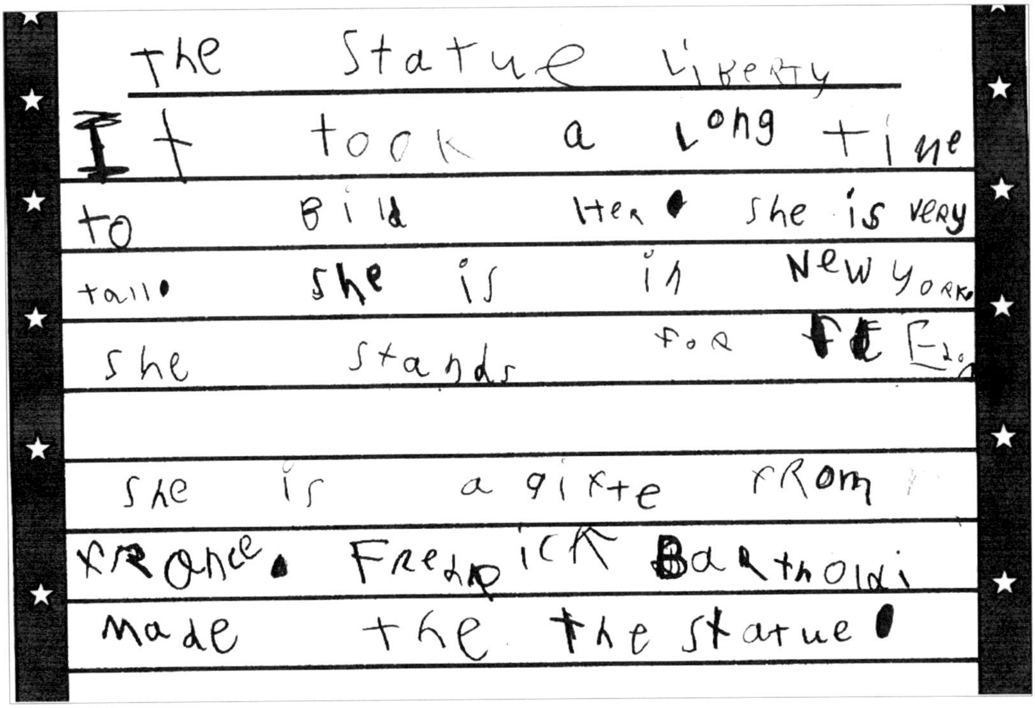

Fig. 12.32

This piece reads:
> *The Statue Liberty*
> *It took a long time to build her. She*
> *is very tall. She is in New York.*
> *She stands for freedom. She is a*
> *gift from France. Fredrick Bartholdi*
> *Made the statue.*

We save the best for last. At the conclusion of this study unit, each child writes a letter to the President, which I always mail. We begin with a discussion of what we might like to say to the President, now that we have learned such a great deal about America. I stress the importance of telling the President something interesting. I ask the students to think about

Kim Dumaine

the idea of receiving an interesting letter rather than a boring letter. The students have an opportunity to share ideas with the class. I will list a few of their ideas on the board in order to aid their memory later, when they begin writing. The children may also look back into their journals for ideas. I create American Flag stationary for the kids to use. Here are a few samples of their letters to the President (Figs. 12/35-12.36).

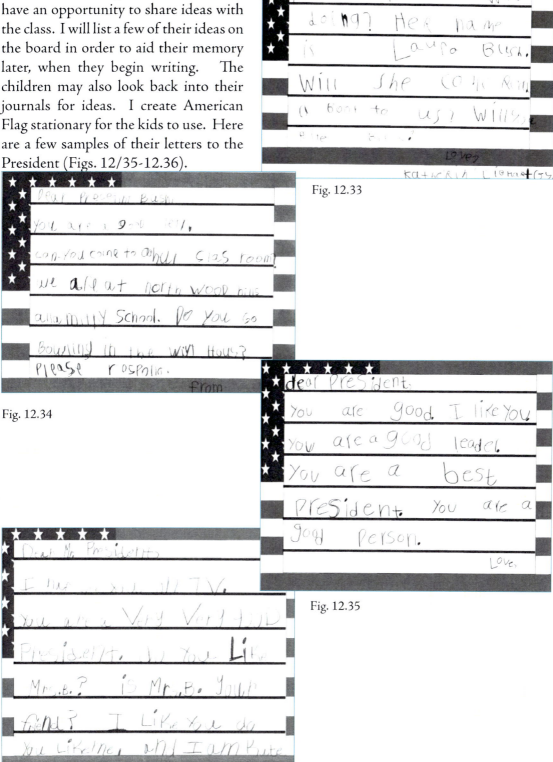

Fig. 12.33

Fig. 12.34

Fig. 12.35

Fig. 12.36

The reward for the students is fantastic. The President has never failed to write back to my class. He usually also includes gifts such as picture postcards or 8x10 photographs. The children are thrilled when this package arrives. It is always so exciting to receive these packages —nothing sets up meaning and purpose for writing quite like receiving a letter from the president of the United States (especially when one is five years old.)

Yet another social studies concept taught in kindergarten is map reading. And what better way to learn map reading than map-making? I begin by showing "grown up" maps to the children, and by reading **Me On the Map** by Joan Sweeney. Next we take a walk around the school with a camera in hand. The photos taken around the school can be used to create a poster-sized map of the school. Of course this map (Fig. 12.37) is labeled using Interactive Writing.

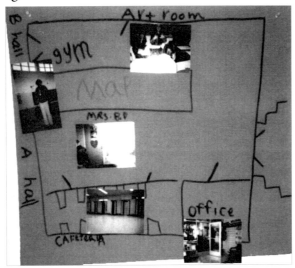

Fig. 12.37

Later in the school year we take a trip to the local zoo. We take map-making a step further this time, by creating a key to go along with our map. The names of the animals on the key are written using Interactive Writing, and the kids cut out pictures of the appropriate animals from magazines to place in each area (Fig. 12.32).

Every social studies unit in kindergarten lends itself to writing opportunities. Interactive Writing can be a tool for reviewing learned information, and individual student writing is a great tool for assessing student mastery of information. Writing helps to offer children a sense of pride, in that it gives them a way to "show off" what they have learned in Social Studies. This builds confidence in children, and in turn, encourages them to continue to grow as young writers.

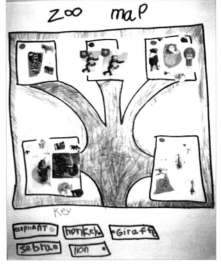

Fig. 12.32

Writing in Math

Writing is an important component in the teaching of math at the kindergarten level. It is through the use of writing that true comprehension can be determined. The use of language takes our math skills to a higher level cognitively, and allows for math to be applied to daily life. When I apply math to the daily lives of my kindergarten students, they are able to see the need for math and to absorb it on a personal level. They begin to enjoy math. When my students are invested in a subject or a task, they naturally put forth their best effort. In my opinion, writing helps to make math even more fun and exciting than it already is! This is a small sampling of only a few cases in which writing can be used in kindergarten math. Good teachers use writing in their kindergarten math lessons almost daily, and here are a couple of chances to do just that.

One of the first concepts taught in the kindergarten math curriculum is that of position words. This is a skill involving the use of vocabulary, so writing fits right in. ***Rosie's Walk*** by Pat Hutchkins is a favorite read-aloud, and it makes for a wonderful introduction to the concept of position words. This book tells the story of a hen on a walk through a farm, and it makes uses of position words along the way. Following the reading of this story, I broke the students up into four groups of five students, so they could create partial retellings, using the position words that are found in this story. This also served as a sort of early version of Blueprinting, since each child in the group took part in the project. For the project, each group was asked to create a mural, with both illustration and text, depicting the position words involved in that particular section of the story. The children were given art materials, such as construction paper and markers, as well as sentence strips for writing. As this takes place very early in the school year, the students needed guidance and direction throughout the entire process. The children first created the mural using the supplies offered. The next step was to add text, such as *above*, *over*, and *on top*. I roamed around the room to offer assistance as the children wrote out their position words, or prepositional phrases. Each child also wrote a first name on a sentence strip, which was added to the project. Since this was our first group project, I paid attention to the groups that were able to work cohesively together. I also noted the students that still needed to fine tune their people skills. These mental notes prove to be helpful to me through the remainder of the year.

Upon completion, each group shared their work with the class, and these murals were placed in a center so that the children could act out the story, practicing their position words. For our first group project, I was pleased with the learning and group interaction that took place. This was a beginning for my children; there would be many more times my kids would need to work together as a team on a group-writing project. I do this particular activity as an introduction to group writing (Figs.

Fig. 12.39

Fig. 12.40

Fig. 12.41

Fig. 12.42

12.39-12.42) because the goals can be clearly defined and easily understood by my students.

Another beginning of the year kindergarten math concept is shapes. We begin with two-dimension shapes and move on to three-dimensional shapes at a later point in the school year. During the study of two-dimensional shapes, we began each day's math lesson with Interactive Writing. Each day for one week, we construct a simple sentence about shapes using Word Wall Words, such as *can* and *see*. As a child comes up to chart paper to write out a word in the sentence, the rest of the class writes along on their white boards. On the last day of the week, we create the front cover for our shapes book, *We Can See Shapes* (Figs. 12.43 & 12.44). The students were invited to circle the Word Wall Words found in the book, which is a predictable pattern book that uses the same Word Wall Words on each page.

The students each are able to contribute further by adding an illustration to each

Fig. 12.43

Fig. 12.44

page using markers. After binding the pages of the book together, it was read and re-read through shared reading, until it was placed into the math center to be enjoyed as the children so desired.

Much later in the school year, the students create a similar predictable book, through Interactive Writing, displaying three-dimensional shapes (FIGS. 12.45 & 12.46). This time, however, the Word Wall Words that are utilized are a little bit more challenging, such as *these* and *are*. Additionally, the students no longer have the desire to circle Word Wall Words when they are found in modeled writing. Also, the children do not create the illustrations in this book. Instead, the children search for three-dimensional shapes in magazines. This helps me in my assessment of the children's understanding about the differences between two-dimensional shapes and three-dimensional shapes.

Fig. 12.36

Growth can be seen from the first shapes book to the second. The children are more knowledgeable about capitalization within a sentence, penmanship has improved, and confidence has increased.

The One-Hundredth Day of School is a big milestone in any

Fig. 12.36

kindergarten classroom. It affords opportunities for writing as well. In his journal (Fig. 12.47), one child decided to share his knowledge about the coins that make up one dollar, as they are studied daily during calendar.

This serves as a tool for me to assess this child's understanding of coins and coin value. Yet another child chose to write about "What he would do with one hundred dollars." This is a common activity in many classrooms on this special day.

Upon examination, I found that this child had, in fact, written about amounts that would total exactly one hundred dollars. Again, this piece of writing helps me to ascertain the comprehension of math lessons that were taught in the classroom. These types of 'one hundred day writing' can take place during writer's workshop or during center time, or even during the math block, depending upon the desires of the teacher and the abilities of the students.

Following the One Hundredth Day of School, I realize that I have many small items of food left over from creating our One Hundred Day Trail Mix, such as small candies, nuts, or cereal pieces. This provided us with another chance to combine math and writing. I gave each

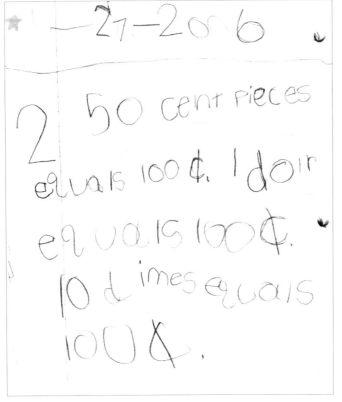

Fig. 12.47

of my students die-cut hands and encouraged them to create addition problems using the left over food items (Figs. 12.49 & 12.50). The children explain their addition problems using a number sentence and words, so that the reader is able to identify the type of food. My students enjoy this activity a great deal, as they were able to have control and make choices in their writing. Not only are they able to choose their food, but they are also in charge of the amounts that they use in their addition problems. For some of my students, editing is part of the fun. No small amount of the white *mistake tape* is used on a few of these pages, which are later compiled into an "addition book".

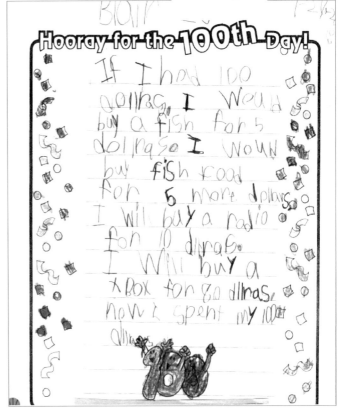

Fig. 12.48

Fig. 12.49

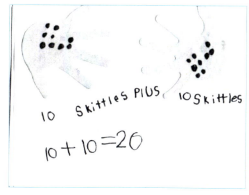

Fig. 12.50

A few weeks after the One Hundredth Day, we use writing to graph (Figs. 12.51) predictions about Groundhog's Day. As a class, we set our purpose by asking a yes or no question, to be answered after watching the news to determine the Groundhog's behavior: "Did the groundhog see his shadow?"

The students chart out their answers as "yes, no" or "I don't know," as they enter the classroom the morning of the newscast. After all of the kids graph their guesses, we total each possible choice and write sentences about what we notice. One thing that we notice is that the most popular answer is not always the correct answer. Only five of the people thought that the groundhog saw his shadow, which he did. A whopping fourteen children thought otherwise. However,

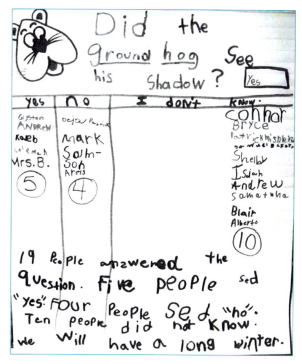

Fig. 12.51

we all enjoy writing about this topic and graphing the outcome. And making observations about graphs is an important math skill, which is tested on our district math assessments. Writing observations out on charts serves my children well. They are able to refer to these charts many times throughout the school year to double check their skills as they come across questions. These charts are a useful resource, and have greater meaning when children create them, rather than using store bought graphs and charts.

Graphing everyday objects provides students with a real-life opportunity to write about their observations in math (Fig. 12.52). For this lesson, I give each of three children a

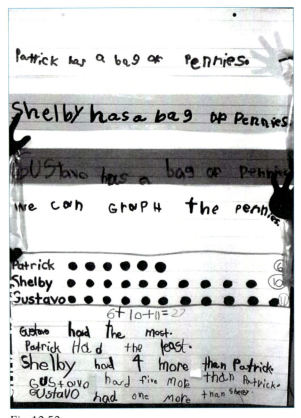

Fig. 12.52

baggie of pennies. As a class, we begin by writing three sentences about the pennies: "Patrick has a bag of pennies. Shelby has a bag of pennies. Gustavo has a bag of pennies." We then attach each bag of pennies to a die-cut hand shape, and staple them to the corresponding sentences. I ask my students what they would like to do during math with these pennies. We agree to graph the pennies first, so we write out that idea interactively: We can graph the pennies. As the kids count the pennies in each bag, I draw the brown circles for the graph. Next, we use Interactive Writing to record our observations:

> Gustavo had the most.
> Patrick had the least.
> Shelby had four more than Patrick.
> Gustavo had five more than Patrick.
> Gustavo had one more than Shelby.

The following day, I ask the students if we could do anything else with these pennies during math. We decide we can add the pennies. After the students come up and write the equation interactively, we realize that we have never worked an addition problem of this difficulty, so we brainstorm how to come up with the solution. One child offers the idea of dumping out all of the pennies and counting them. Piggybacking off that idea, another child notices that we can simply count the pennies (brown circles) that we had graphed the previous day. This is the idea that we utilize to find our sum. We mount this chart in the classroom, so we can refer to it as often as we need to during later math lessons.

Using writing to map out thinking processes, children in kindergarten can tackle difficult problem solving, including division, or separating items into equal parts. As an introduction to fractions, we experiment with cutting bread into equal halves. We decide to write about our findings, as the children naturally discover varied forms of equal halves. Some of the children use a diagonal cut to separate the bread into two equal parts, some of the children cut the bread side to side, and some of the children cut the bread top to bottom. The students record results in journals, as can be seen here.

Zachary, a new student in my class, jumps right in to writing beside his peers. His entry reads:

> *We had a big piece of bread. We cut the bread*
> *in half. We had a piece of paper. We drawed*
> *a picture of our bread. I cut my piece of bread*
> *to top to bottom.*

Kindergarteners also learn concepts about parts of a whole through creating and solving their own word problems. I invite the children to take part in the creation of their own fraction situations, which are recorded and shared with classmates. Here is an example created by Connor during this activity (Figs. 12.53 & 12.53).

Because of the level of understanding the students exhibit; I want to challenge the students with a fractional problem of increased length and difficulty. This time, we expand our thinking beyond two equal parts. I begin this lesson by bringing fifteen connecting cubes to the front of the class, along with a small school bus with wheels. On the chart paper, I draw the picture of the "store" and the "house" (Fig. 12.55). This picture is level with the tiny shelf on my easel, so the children are able to "drive" the school bus along this edge. Next, I present the problem to my students verbally. I write the first sentence on the chart myself. "We have 15 cubes." The students write the sentence, "the bus can carry 3 cubes." This is completed using Interactive Writing, and I participate myself, adding the word "carry."

I also add the question, "How many trips will the bus take from the store to the house?" The next step is to actually work out the problem. The students have a great deal of fun both loading and driving the school bus from the store to the house, using the edge of

Fig. 12.53

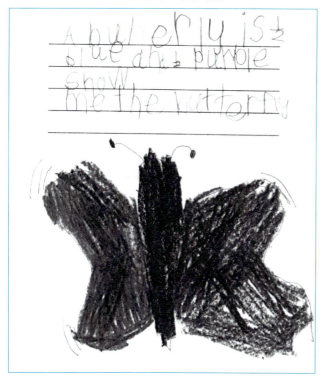

Fig. 12.54

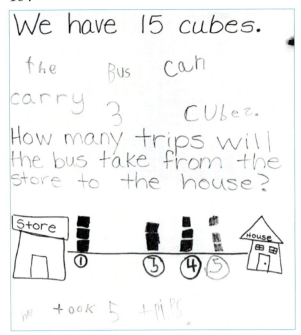

Fig. 12.52

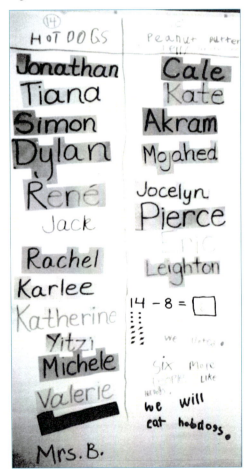

Fig. 12.56

the easel as the road. As they make each trip, they record it, and the cubes that are used. Upon completion of the trips, the children use Interactive Writing to offer the solution to the problem. "We took 5 trips." Activities like this help children to think as a group and use higher-level thinking. This is fun for teacher and student alike.

Voting is another fun way to get children to combine writing with math. During a social studies unit on America, we held our own version of voting in our classroom. We vote on a special lunch: would we eat hot dogs, or peanut butter and jelly sandwiches? (Fig. 12.56)

In order to make this process seem more real, I make "voter's cards" for the kids, which are nothing more than their names written by me on colored paper. I read the kids a story about voting and elections from the *Let's See* book series, called *Voting and Elections*. We discuss new learning from the book, such as standing in line quietly while waiting to vote, and then I draw the T-chart on the graph paper. The students write the names of their preferred lunch items at the top of the T-chart. For the next step, the kids stand in line, just like adults do, and wait to cast their "votes." Upon completion of the voting, we create a subtraction problem to describe the amount of votes on each side of the T-chart. Then the children write out their observations. "We voted. Six more people like hotdogs. We will eat hotdogs." Teachers conduct voting activities in their kindergarten classrooms all the time. Adding a writing component helps the children to understand the thinking pattern (subtraction) involved in a voting activity, which adds to their comprehension of this process.

One concept that can be quite difficult for kindergarten students is that of telling time. Telling time is complicated, and requires thinking about more than one concept simultaneously. The young child must be able to be aware of the difference between the hour hand and the minute hand, count by fives, and/or be able to add, all at the same moment. Writing about telling time aids the mental comprehension of this difficult task. We sit down as a class and discuss the difficulties of understanding the clock and how it works, following several previous lessons. (During these earlier lessons, the children practiced telling time with manipulative clocks and interactive toy clocks, which helped the children to learn how to tell time.) It is important for my kids to be able to "talk out" the telling time intricacies before we begin to write them out. This helps to avoid any confusion or disagreements about the steps that are recorded. Additionally, it is important that we keep our thoughts short and concise. Following our discussion, the kids write out the steps involved in telling time interactively (Fig. 12.57). They also decide to include a visual with their writing, so we add the illustration of the clock face. I reflect that this is a wise decision on the part of the students. This graphic and step-by-step instructional piece helps my students a great deal. We hang in it the classroom and make use of this visual many times during math instruction. Because the children created these instructions themselves, it holds much more meaning than anything that I could have purchased at a teacher store. This was the first time that I had ever invited one of my kindergarten classes to consider writing out their own directions to help in the learning of the telling time

Fig. 12.52

process. I learned from my students that young children are highly capable if given the opportunity. Because of the amount of experience that they have with group work and with writing, they are very successful in describing a difficult concept. This reminds me that as a teacher I need to be certain that I am offering my students every chance to be confident, independent thinkers.

    The ability to comprehend the problem-solving processes of mathematical equations requires knowing how to take apart the equations and explain the steps needed to come to a solution. This is a tall order for a five year old. It is so important that teachers model this process as often as possible. My elementary campus uses a strategy called U.P.S.Check to help the students to understand the problem solving process. The premise is that the kids first Understand the problem, then Plan out the thinking pattern to use, followed by showing the way to Solve the problem, and finally, Checking the work. This process is all about writing and using a graphic organizer.

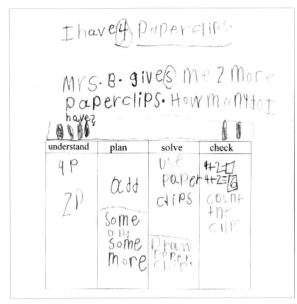

Fig. 12.58

I introduce this strategy using Modeled Writing, Shared Writing and Interactive Writing, because I know my kids have a comfort level in this arena, and I believe some comfort is helpful when introducing a new concept (Fig. 12.58). I generate an addition word problem making use of students in a classroom, because I know that this is something the children can relate to. I explain the U.P.S. Check process to the students and draw out the graphic organizer. For the Understand section, I ask the children to use initials to save time, to notice "the important information that we need to understand," and to observe that we have a question to answer. The "3B" stands for three boys, and the "1g" stands for one girl. Next we Plan. We know that this is an addition problem, because the thinking pattern involved is "some and some more." We discuss two possible ways to Solve this equation. The children decide to "act it out" and to "use cubes." For the Check portion, we write out the problem in equation form, and then repeat the same equation, with proof.

I realize that the students need more exposure to this new way of thinking about working equations, and that they also need more practice as a whole group before attempting this process individually. To accomplish this is a non-threatening manner, I incorporate U.P.S. Check into our math lessons as a wrap up activity at the conclusion of each math lesson, over a couple of days' time.

As we are studying about trees and leaves in science, I decide to integrate this into our U.P.S. Check equation at the conclusion of a math lesson. I begin by asking the children if they would like to create an addition problem using leaves. The kids help to choose the color of the leaves and the amount of each color involved in the word problem, which I write at the top of the chart paper using Shared Writing (Fig. 12.59).

Next I draw out the graphic organizer below the word problem as the kids look on. For the Understand portion, I invite the students to raise a hand if they wish to come up and document the important

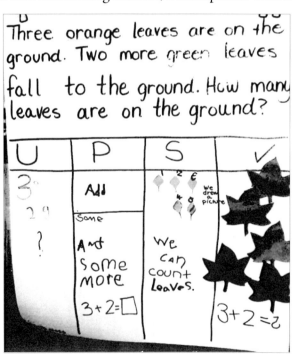

Fig. 12.59

information that we understand about the problem. Three different children come up to fill in this part of the graphic organizer. For the Plan portion, we discuss what type of problem this might be. One student comes up to write the word "add," and the kids use Interactive Writing to include the thinking pattern, "some and some more." One of the ways we decide to Solve the problem is to use the strategy of drawing the leaves, which the children do, using the colors mentioned in the word problem. After drawing the leaves and numbering the leaves, the students use Interactive Writing to add the sentence, "We can count leaves." We use actual die-cut leaves to Check our work. The children tape the leaves under the Check portion of the organizer, number them, and write out the equation under the leaves.

We also happen to be learning about various Presidents in social studies, which includes information as to which currency we find various Presidents' faces. Young children truly enjoy working with money, so I make use of coins in an U.P.S. Check subtraction word problem. I chose a child in the class to be the main character. I use modeled writing to create this word problem in front of the class (Fig. 12.60).

I then draw the graphic organizer below the word problem. As before, students come up and write out what is Understood from the initial reading of this word problem. The students realize that this is a subtraction problem because some pennies were given away. We use interactive writing to document "subtract,"

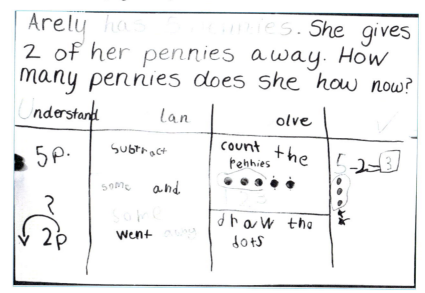

Fig. 12.60

and "some and some went away" for the thinking pattern under the Plan component. For the Solve portion, of course the children want to use actual pennies, which we have plenty of in our classroom. So the students again use Interactive Writing, along with actual pennies, in order to plot out two ways to Solve this word problem. Under the Check portion, the students create an appropriate equation and Check their work by drawing dots to represent the pennies.

Now that the kids have experiences using the UPS Check strategy for solving word problems, they are ready to attempt this method individually. The children are given blank paper, with only the graphic organizer in place. They can now create their own word problems to be solved using the UPS Check method, which I can use to assess understanding. Here are three student samples of individual work, completed by three different students (Fig 12.61-12.63). This is also a great tool for the math center. Students can go into math center and write out word problems for their friends to attempt. Using this method causes children to use their own metacognition skills. Thinking about their own thought processes provides young children with an increased value about the learning that is taking place. This is something we all desire for our students. I know I want all of my kindergarteners to be motivated by the desire to learn, and to place value on their own understanding.

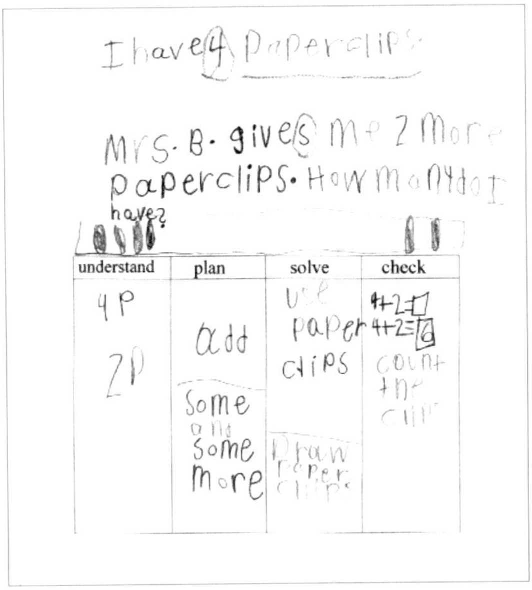

Using writing to hone math skills is a benefit to both teacher and student. Students are provided with another avenue to increase understanding of a task or problem. Teachers are provided with a rich source to decipher the level of understanding that each child holds.

Writing in math can also be differentiated to accommodate for all levels of learners. Some students may simply be asked to turn an equation into a one or two sentence story problem. Still others can create multi-step word problems that relate to a certain topic or study unit. The possibilities are limitless! Best of all, using writing in math gives children yet another opportunity to apply their learning to daily situations that carry real meaning for them.

Fig. 12.61

Fig. 12.62

Fig. 12.63

13. Publishing and Celebrating

Publishing in kindergarten must be accomplished with a delicate hand. I must know my students well before we can proceed into publishing together.

For me, publishing takes place only after the child's piece has been drafted, and the child is happy with his or her draft. This means that content conferencing has already taken place, in depth. The child has read and re-read the piece, made deletions (which occurs rarely), and additions (which occurs often), added details, read to peers to hear the sound of the piece read aloud, and of course, conferenced with me. At this point we can begin what we call "editing" in our classroom.

Editing refers to the conventions for which a particular child is responsible. And every child in my class is not responsible for the same conventions; thus, the need for me to know each child extremely well. I also need to be aware how much editing each child can handle emotionally. It is important that each child maintains a healthy attitude about his or her piece and about the editing process. As Carol Avery says in ***…And with a Light Touch***, "It's important not to overload the writer so I choose what to address depending on my sense of how much the writer can handle"(107)

As far as naming some of the conventions that are edited in my classroom, we do attack capitalization and punctuation. Capitalization corrections are fairly easy for the student to locate, as a new sentence begins directly after the punctuation mark from the previous sentence. The children have been taught from the beginning that, "A capital letter always comes at the beginning of a sentence." The other situation that calls for capital use in my kindergarten is the beginning of a name. Capitalization is a good starting place for beginning editors, since the corrections are so easy to find. Punctuation can be a little bit trickier.

Here is a little strategy that I employ from the very beginning of the school year that helps my children to identify the ends of sentences both in reading and in writing. I teach the children to make a little sound whenever they see a period, "hmm." It sounds silly, but it works. I introduce this idea using Big Books with large print, so that the students can clearly see the "hmm" at the end of a sentence. We do call it a period as well, when we are discussing the punctuation mark. But when reading aloud, we simply say "hmm" when we come across this little dot at the end of a sentence. Next, I continue to make the sound when I model my own writing. As I read each sentence aloud, I include a "hmm" at the end of each sentence. I encourage the kids to do the same during Interactive Writing. This is a little silly, but it is great fun for the children, and soon they develop an ear for the exact spot where a sentence should end. This makes my life easier during editing conferences. I ask the child to read the piece to me aloud, and as they come to the end of a sentence, they naturally say "hmm." If no period appears in this spot, I rarely need to make note of the lacking period to the young writer, as they just heard the sound come out of their own mouth! The child almost automatically picks up the pencil and adds the period!

As far as corrections involving spelling, this also depends greatly upon the child. I hold my children responsible only for correctly spelling the Word Wall Words (and words in Word Banks) and even then, I only hold those kids responsible whom I know have mastered all of the Word Wall Words. And I want the writers to locate these words independently in their writing. So I ask the writer to read the piece, strictly looking for Word Wall Words. I ask the child to circle the Word Wall Words in his or her own writing. This is a common request for me to make of all of the children during any stage of their writing, so it is no big deal to the child at this point. The beauty of this strategy, again, is that the child takes charge. Most of the time the child will notice the spelling of the Word Wall Word the moment it is circled. This eliminates the need for teacher correction. However, sometimes I may need to draw a child's attention to a certain Word Wall Word, even after it has been circled. All I need to do is ask the child to locate that word on the Word Wall, and the child makes the mental connection. I believe it is far better for the child to control as much of the editing as possible. I want to avoid creating writers that are constantly dependent on adult correction. Rather, I want my students to have an "I can" spirit that they can rely on throughout life.

A big part of the publishing stage that is exciting for the children is the creation of a title for their piece. I encourage the students to save this for the very end, as a reward one gives to one's self. Often the title chosen by the young writer is not one that I may agree with. This is okay. It is good for me to remember that I do not have to like the title, since it not my piece. This helps me as a teacher to remember that my wish is for the writers to feel power and control over their own work—not me.

Many times the young writer will also want to illustrate their work, and this is part of the publishing stage as well. I leave this choice up to the student. If the student desires illustrations, I say, "Go for it." If the child does not feel like illustrating the work, that is great too. Usually the piece will be mounted on card stock or construction paper, placed into a book form with a cover, or highlighted in some special format that lets the child know that this work is special.

The fun begins when the work is celebrated. The child reads his or her work the class, and takes questions and comments. But it is also fun to invite the child to read this piece to other adults around the school. I am blessed that both office personnel, and other classroom teachers at Northwood Hills Elementary are happy to listen to my young authors. Equally special is allowing my kindergarten writers to read to their older siblings in other classrooms. This must be prearranged with the teacher of the older sibling, but most teachers are very happy to accommodate.

At my school, we have one form of extreme publishing, which we call The Writer's Assembly. Four times during the school year we have a School Wide Writing Day. Prior to this day, the entire school writes in their own individual classrooms. We usually all write to the same very broad topic, although not always. If we do use a topic, it will be something every child can relate to, such as writing about a time we lost something or writing about the first day of school.

Everyone writes, whether they write to the topic or not. The children may take their pieces through the entire writing process, if they so choose. The classroom teacher will then select one piece to celebrate by inviting the author to read this piece to the principal at The Writer's Assembly, in front of the entire school. This is a day that is anticipated by the children in my classroom with great joy and eagerness. Parents are invited as well. We do not run into problems of jealousy because we are a community that loves and supports one another. My students are always genuinely happy for the child that reads at this assembly. The children also know that there will always be another chance to be a reader because there is always another assembly coming soon. Of course, teachers talk to each other across classrooms and grade levels in order to avoid choosing the same author repetitively. This requires only a small amount of effort on the part of the teachers, and the reward is great to the children. By keeping track of previous readers so that we do not repeat, a greater number of authors have the chance to participate in this experience. It is truly a joyful day for every child, and more importantly, it models to the children that writing is valued at our school. Pictured is a student from my classroom at one of these assemblies, seen posing with me, (Fig. 13.1) as well as with the school principal, Kyle Stuard (Fig. 13.2).

Fig. 13.1

Fig. 13.2

To the teacher that would like to implement such an occasion in his or her own school: Know that it is no easy task to convince your staff and leadership that this is a valuable activity, especially today, when constant testing takes precedence over any time spent writing. Not only is this program work to implement, but it is also work to maintain. It is all too easy for a school to become "too busy" for yet another assembly. The teacher that begins this program needs to be strong and persistent about continuing to hold School Wide Writing Days and Assemblies. My blessing came by way of my Instructional Specialist on my campus, Kim Whitfield, who holds to the same philosophy as I do – that writing in the elementary school is vital. She made these days important to the staff and the children. She helped me in my pursuit to give writing value. She became the face of The Writer's Assembly, and for that I owe her many thanks. This program would not have been successful without Kim Whitfield. So, to the teacher intending to start up such a program, I suggest, you get help from your teammates, your best teacher friend, or your principal, but do enlist the help of a teaching partner. The joy on the faces of the students after that first Writer's Assembly is priceless. Sharing the joy of writing with students, coworkers, and parents is a gift that continues giving to all.

14 Assessment

Rubrics

    Rubrics are a great way to assess kindergarten writing. These examples show the same rubric being used to grade five student's different writing samples, which take place over the course of the school year. Using one rubric to assess the same child's writing at varied times throughout the year is an easy and convenient way to show the progress of each individual student. This type of rubric is also a wonderful instrument to use in conferencing with parents. The rubrics that are shown use kindergarten TEKS as the components to be assessed. Some teachers may prefer to use another source as the components that will be included in each rubric. (I suggest meeting as a grade level team to decide the components that are important to you and your students as you determine a rubric to assess your students' progress as writers.)

    The rubrics shown are used on my campus to assess the writings of our students on School Wide Writing Day. On this day, every child in the school writes. Students in kindergarten through sixth grade celebrate authorship by writing as a unified campus. Later, one child in each classroom will read their piece at an assembly in front of the entire school. This has been a ritual in my school for the past five years. It is truly a celebration that the children look forward to.

    Grade level teachers meet as a team to assess student writing. Meeting together insures that all teachers adhere to the same standard when assessing with rubrics. It also helps to lessen the subjectivity that may occur when a single teacher is assessing student writing.

    These rubrics are saved and then passed on to the next year's teacher. This continues all the way up to sixth grade, at which time each student's portfolio of rubrics and samples are passed on to the junior high or sent home to the parents as a record of the student's growth from the age of five to the age of twelve.

    It is important to attach the actual writing sample to the rubric that is being used for assessment. This eliminates any confusion for future teachers (or parent) viewing the work of the child.

The indicators that are used in this particular rubric are: LS for lacking skill, NI for needs improvement, I for improving, and M for mastery. We have more recently started using numbers as indicators (1,2,3,4) in order to align our grading with the assessment style used by the state. By using numbers, the students will be familiar with the type of grading they will face in fourth grade on the Writing Test. Also more recently, we have re-worked some of the items on the rubric to contain more information about content (see Sasha's rubric Fig. 14.1), rather than having the entire assessment cover mechanics only. The new rubric includes "Writes to record ideas, K15,c" and "Ideas show connections, K16b." It was important that content be included in this new rubric, as content is actually far more important than mechanics at this early stage.

Kindergarten Writing Portfolio Checklist
2002-2003

Student: Sasha   **Special Services:** esl

Teacher: Dumaine

School-wide Writing dates:	Narr. Sept. 18	Retell Nov. 22	Letter Feb. 27	How To May 7
Attempts letter formation (K14.B)	M	M	M	M
Writes Name (K14A)	I	M	M	M
Phonological Knowledge (K.14C)	NI	I	I+	I++
Uses word wall (K.14A)	M	M	M	M
Begins to use capitals and punctuation correctly (K.5F)	I	I+	M	M
Writes to record ideas (K.15C)	I	M	M	M
Knowledge that written words are separated by spacing (K.5C)	I	M	M	M
Left to right movement (K14D)	I	M	M	M
Ideas show connections (K.16B)	M	M	M	M

COMMENTS:
_____
_____
_____
_____

SCORING: LS (lacking skill) NI (needs improvement) I (improving) M (mastery)
Please place one of these scores in each cell for the type of writing you are evaluating

Fig. 14.1

Kim Dumaine

Shasha's work scored on the rubric:

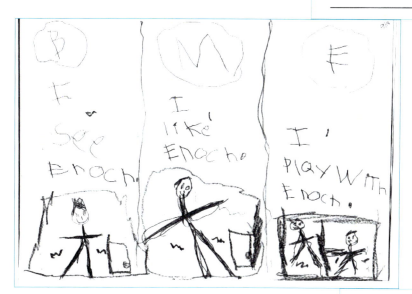

Again, these are local choices, best made by each school, or even each grade level team. Keep your assessment rubrics, or analytic scales, workable for your students and your situation. Of course it is ideal to be able to work as a team with your entire staff. But remember, it always begins on a campus because one individual teacher is doing something right that works for kids. Somebody has to get things started —why not you?

I meet with the parents of each student twice during the school year to discuss each child's progress as a writer. These samples, along with the rubrics, provide evidence of student growth in a concrete form that parents can understand and appreciate. Rubrics make sense to the parents of my students. Not only do they show areas of growth, but they also offer goals to move toward. Parents appreciate having this knowledge about their children. I notice that after conducting these conferences, my students begin to come to school with stories that they authored at home. I believe this is due to greater understanding on the part of the parents. Now that the parents are celebrating writing at home, the young authors are bubbling over with stories! Parents are thrilled that they can be a part of the process. Witnessing a young child blossom into an independent writer is a miraculous experience.

Closing

The experience of documenting a small portion of this last year's writing lessons has truly been a joy for me. I have sincerely been able to view the growth of my students from an enlightened point of view. I loved watching my students grow, learning from my mistakes, gaining ideas and insights from my students, and learning side by side with my kindergarteners. I see the power of knowing my students well. I see the power of giving young writers both freedom and responsibility.

Beliefs that I have always applied in my classroom have now become concrete and real because I have had to analyze cause and effect. The reality is before me. Young children can write and write well. They can be passionate, gifted writers. They can have purpose and meaning when they write. Teachers who know their students have the ability to open them up to the gifts that they possess. No scripted literacy adoption can do what knowledgeable teachers can do.

We have all read books that discuss the need for teachers to work with the students, and not the adoption. I used to read those same books, and wonder why the authors stressed this point over and over again... "I get it," I used to think.

Seeing my students' work before me, I truly do "get it." And so did all those knowledgeable authors, urging us to meet the needs of our students and not the agendas of others. "Be true to your students," they would charge. Now I am charging right along with them. This book has provided me with the evidence that young children are capable of thinking, exploring, writing, and understanding. This is a craft they need to learn from their teachers, not mandated by someone who does not know their name.

Young children learn in a safe, loving, environment that fosters risk-taking and independent thinking. This environment can only be provided by us, the classroom teachers. I have faith that a change is in the works. I believe in teachers. I see talented teachers working with the students they care about every day. We all know these teachers. They are dedicated to their young authors and stand behind them. These teachers will not sacrifice Writer's Workshop for mandated worksheets. These are the teachers who cultivate independent thinkers and promote best practices. These are the teachers who put their students first. I want to be one of these teachers.

 References

Adler, D. 1998. *A Picture book of Abraham Lincoln.* New York. NY: Holiday House.
_____. 1998. *A Picture book of George Washington.* New York. NY: Holiday House.
Anderson, C. 2000. *How's It Going?* Portsmouth. NH: Heinemann.
Anton, W. 1999. *Where Does the Water Go?* New York. NY. Newbridge Educational Publishing.
Avery, C. 2002. *…And with a Light Touch: Learning About Reading, Writing, and Teaching With First Graders.* Portsmouth. NH: Heinemann.
Beil, K. 1998. *A Cake All for Me.* New York. NY: Holiday House.
Bissex, G. 1980. *GYNS AT WORK, A Child Learns to Write and Read.* Cambridge. MA: Harvard University Press.
Bissex, G., and Bullock, R. 1987. *SEEING FOR OURSEVES, Case-Study Research by Teachers of Writing.* Portsmouth. NH: Heinemann.
Branley, F. 1997. *Down Comes the Rain.* New York. NY: Harper Collins Publishers.
Bridwell, N. 1997. *Clifford's First Valentine's Day.* New York. NY: Scholastic Inc.
Briggs, R. 1990. *The Snowman Storybook.* New York. NY: Random House.
Brown, M. 1989. *Arthur's Birthday.* Boston. MA: Joy Street Books.
_____. 1992. *Arthur Meets The President.* Boston. MA: Joy Street Books.
Buehner, C. 2002. *Snowmen at Night.* New York. NY: Phyllis Fogelman Books.
Burns, M. 1995. *Writing In Math Class.* Sausalito, CA: Math Solutions Publications.
Cambourne, B. and Brown, H. 1990. *Read and Retell: A Strategy for the Whole Language/ Natural Learning Classroom.* Portsmouth. NH: Heinemann.
Carlson, N. 1990. *I Like Me!* New York. NY: Puffin Books.
_____. *How To Lose All Your Friends.* New York. NY: Viking.
_____. *Look Out Kindergarten, Here I Come!* New York. NY: Penguin Putnam Books for Young Readers.
Carroll, J. A. and Wilson, E. 1993. *ACTS of Teaching: How to Teach Writing.* Englewood. CA: Teacher Ideas Press.
Carroll, J.A. and Wilson, E. "Benchmarking: The Result of a State of Fear." *Reflexive and Extensive Journal* (Fall 2005/Winter2006): 5-6.
Cowen- Fletcher, J. 1993. *Mama Zooms.* New York. NY: Scholastic Inc.

Cronin, D. 2004. *Duck for President*. New York. NY: Simon & Schuster Books for Young.

Cuyler, M. 1998. *The Biggest, Best Snowman*. New York. NY: Scholastic.

DePaola, T. 1996. *The Baby Sister*. New York. NY: Putnam's Son.

Dixon-Krass, L. 1996. *Vygotsky in the Classroom, Mediated Literacy Instruction and Assessment*. White Plains. NY: Longman Publishers.

Donaldson, M. 1978. *Children's Minds*. New York. NY: W.W. Norton & Company.

Dorn, L. et.al. 1998. *Apprenticeship in Literacy: Transitions Across Reading and Writing*. York. MA: Stenhouse Publishers.

Dorn, L. and Soffos, C. 2001. *Scaffolding Young Writers: A Writer's Workshop Approach*. Portland. ME: Stenhouse Publishers.

Drazin, S. 1995. *Writing Math*. Glenview. IL: Good Year Books.

Eagle, K. 1999. *Humpty Dumpty*. Dallas, TX: Whispering Coyote Press.

Ehlert, L. 1995. *Snowballs*. San Diego. CA: Harcourt Brace.

Fisher, B. *Joyful Learning in Kindergarten*. 1998. Portsmouth. NH: Heinemann.

Gentry, R. *Spel…Is A Four-Letter Word*. 1987. Portsmouth. NH: Heinemann.

Gray, S. 2002. *The White House*. Minneapolis. MN: Compass Point Books.

Gibbs, J. 2001. *Tribes: A New Way of Learning and Being Together*. Windsor. CA: Center Source Systems, LLC.

Harris, Jim. 1997. *Jack and the Giant: A Story Full of Beans*. Flagstaff. AZ. Northland Publishing.

Hest, A. 1995. *In The Rain With Baby Duck*. Cambridge. MA: Candlewick Press.

Hoberman, M. 1997. *The Seven Silly Eaters*. San Diego. CA: Harcourt Brace.

Holabird, K. 1989. *Angelina's Birthday Surprise*. New York. NY: C.N. Potter: Distributed by Crown.

Hutchins, P. 1978. *Happy Birthday, Sam*. New York. NY: Greenwillow Books.

_____. 1987. *Rosie's Walk*. New York. NY: Scholastic.

Jacobs, D. 1999. *Discovery Teams*. New York. NY: Newbridge Educational Publishing.

Johnson, A. 1990. *When I am Old With You*. New York. NY: Orchard Books.

_____. 1995. *One of Three*. New York. NY: Orchard Books.

Kellog, S. 1997. *Jack and the Beanstalk*. New York. NY: Harper Trophy

Kent, J. 1969. *Mr. Elephant's Birthday Party*. Boston. MA: Houghton Mifflin.

Kirk, D. 2000. *Snow Family*. New York. NY: Hyperion Books for Children.

Krosoczka, J. 2004. *Max for President*. New York. NY: Knopf.

Kunhardt, E. 1986. *Danny's Birthday*. New York. NY: Greenwillow Books.

Lanczak Williams, R. 1994. *Rain*. Cypress. CA: Creative Teaching Press Inc.

Locker, T. 1997. *Water Dance*. San Diego. CA: Harcourt Brace & Co.

Maccarone, G. 1992. *The Sword in the Stone*. New York. NY: Scholastic Inc.

Magnuson, K. 1998. *A Cake All For Me*. New York. NY: Holiday House.

Marshall, J. 1993. *Old Mother Hubbard and her Wonderful Dog*. New York, NY: Farrar, Straus, and Girox.

_____. 1987. *Red Riding Hood*. New York. NY: Penguin Group.

Mayer, M. 1985. *Just Grandpa and Me*. Racine. WI: Western Publishing Company, Inc.

McBratney, S. 1995. *Guess How Much I Love You*. Cambridge. MA: Candlewick Press.

McCarrier, A., Pinnell, G.S., and Fountas. Irene C. 2000. *Interactive Writing: How Language and Literacy Come Together.* Portsmouth. NH: Heinemann.

Meachen, D. 2002. *The Statue of Liberty.* Minneapolis. MN: Compass Point Books.

Messenger, N. and Wells, R. 1997. *Jack and the Beanstalk.* Singapore: DK Children.

Murphy, P. J. 2002 *Voting and Elections.* Minneapolis. MN: Compass Point Books.

Newman, J. 2001. *The Craft of Children's Writing.* Spring.TX: Absey & Co., Inc.

Nobelman, M. 2004. *Let's See Book Series.* Minneapolis. MN: Compass Point Books.

Numeroff, L. 2000. *What Daddies Do Best.* New York. NY: Simon & Schuster Books for Young Readers.

_____. 2000 *What Mommies Do Best.* New York. NY: Simon & Schuster Books for Young Readers.

Perrault, C. 1999. *Cinderella.* Verlag, AG. Switzerland: North- South Publishing.

Recht Penner, L. 1995. *The Statue of Liberty.* New York. NY: Random House.

Reid, M. 1995. *How Have I Grown?* New York. NY: Scholastic.

Roberts, D. and Roberts, L. *Cinderella.* New York, NY: Abrams Books

Romay, S. 1994. *Pizza.* New York. NY: Scholastic Inc.

Ryon Quiri, P. 1998. *The Statue of Liberty.* New York. NY: Children's Press.

Sakurai, G. 1995. *The Liberty Bell.* Chicago. IL: Children's Press.

Senisi, E. 1993. *Brothers & Sisters.* New York. NY: Scholastic Inc.

Seuss, Dr. 1959. *Happy Birthday to You!* New York. NY: Random House.

_____. 1988. *Green Eggs and Ham.* New York. NY: Random House.

Shulevitz, U. 1998. *Snow.* New York. NY: Farrar Straus Giroux.

Spinelli, E. 1998. *When Mama Comes Home Tonight.* New York. NY: Simon Schuster Books for Young Readers.

Sweeney, J. 1996. *Me On the Map.* New York. NY: Scholastic Inc.

Velthuijs, M. 1996. *A Birthday Cake for Little Bear.* New York. NY: North-South Books

White, N. 1994. *Happy Birthday, Jesse Bear!* New York. NY: Maxwell Macmillan International.

Whitin, D. and Whitin, P. 2000. *Math is Language Too.* NCTE and NCTM.

Wilde, S. 1992. *You Kan Red This!* Portsmouth, NH: Heinemann.

Wilde, S. and Whitin, D. 1992. *Read Any Good Math Lately?* Portsmouth, NH: Heinemann.

Williams, R. 1994. *Rain.* Cypress. CA: Creative Teaching Press.

Williams, V. 1982. *A Chair for My Mother.* New York. NY: Greenwillow Books.

Winters, K. 2004. *My Teacher for President.* New York. NY: Scholastic Inc.

Yolen, J. 1993. *Mouse's Birthday.* New York. NY: Putnam.

Thanks

No teacher stands alone, nor is successful without gifts received from educational mentors. Many thanks to those teachers who have paved my way: Dr. and Mrs. Guy Harrison, Dr. Joyce Armstrong Carroll, Edward Wilson, Pam Ellard, Kay Frantz, Judy Wilson, Jana Hoffpauir, Rhonda Bybel, Kim Whitfield, Virginia Cotton, Tom and Lucy Fullerton, and Colleen Randall. You all have my deepest respect and gratitude.